THE YEAR OF
THE WORKING TERRIER

(a year in the life of the author's earth dogs)

GW00566799

SEÁN FRAIN

PENNINE PUBLISHING

Pennine Publishing, PO Box 466, Bury, BL8 9BU.

ISBN: 978-0-9552389-1-8

Spring

It had been a hard winter, with severe frost over quite a period of time that left the ground iron-hard and dangerous to walk upon, but now, at last, the days were softening and the daffodils were finally beginning to open, which was most welcome after the drear days of the past few months. Lambing time had begun too and the fields were getting full of bleating little 'woolly-backs', which couldn't get enough of their mothers warm, life-giving milk. But, along with this rapid swell of sheep in the pastures, came troubles which shepherds were just not willing to tolerate – that of foxes taking their newly arrived livestock. And so the lambing calls began to come in, just as I was looking forward to the end of the season.

I telephoned Gary and we soon got together, intent on checking over miles of open countryside where the troubles occurred. This was quite a small farm and we suspected that the culprit may well have been coming in from outlying areas, so we began searching more distant places with my terriers, Rock, Ghyll, Crag and Bella, but each earth and covert we tried just didn't seem to hold. We found the remains of prey outside a brick-lined earth I had known of for years – an unfortunate woodpigeon that wasn't quite quick enough – but, although Ghyll went through the long black tunnel, following the strong scent that betrayed recent occupation, he emerged the other end without finding at home and thus we moved swiftly on with coupled terriers and shotgun close to hand.

As we moved closer to the farm we found more evidence of foxes around the place, yet Reynard was still rather elusive and the lambing troubles continued a couple of days more. The farmer told us of an earth he had discovered nearby and we went to investigate, but it was a freshly dug badger sett and so we marked the spot, keeping well clear with the terriers.

The day was rather cool, but still, I was sweating as we searched the steep pastures and woodland for any sign of our quarry and at last our efforts paid off. We found a previously unknown earth at a rock spot above a small beck, which plunged over the rocks and dropped down towards the river in the valley bottom, and Ghyll keenly marked the spot. This earth was in solid rock and I was a little worried about my terrier getting into trouble here, but

Rock & Bella.

Crag & Ghyll.

it was one of those desperate situations that called for desperate measures and we were determined to end the lamb losses as quickly as possible. With heart in mouth, I loosed Ghyll and he slipped into the earth with little fuss, despite the drop down he had before disappearing among the cold grey boulders. He was only gone for a short time when baying signalled a find and Gary prepared for a bolt, which came soon after, with a medium sized fox shooting out of the earth at great speed and making rapidly across the rough ground. Gary raised his gun, took aim and emptied both barrels, though the first dropped her instantly and I am certain she was dead before hitting the ground.

The shepherd was shown the carcass and he was most pleased, for now the lambing troubles stopped and he carried on his tender care of the newborn and growing lambs without distraction from unwelcome predators. I do not like to kill foxes during the breeding season, in fact, I do not like killing them at all, for they are a beautiful, enchanting animal that ranks among my favourites, but I have grown up seeing first hand the damage foxes can do and control is vital where livestock is reared, or, indeed, where ground-nesting birds raise young. This vixen had no youngsters, but she it was who was the culprit, for the troubles ended abruptly and there was no need to visit that farm again during that particular springtime.

Many puzzle over why foxes kill lambs, often only taking the head and leaving the rest, whilst moving on to attack another, while others say that foxes do not kill lambs at all and only eat stillborn carcasses, but that is fiction of the highest degree. There is no mystery surrounding lamb losses. Foxes are opportunistic hunters and will often kill more than they need when they find themselves in times of plenty, such as at lambing time. They will kill, take the head and often 'cache' it nearby, while killing more. The 'cache' acts as a sort of storehouse for when times are lean again, but very often foxes will forget about this reserve and will not return to it, or another fox will discover and steal it while out foraging. And so lamb losses can be quite serious at this time of year. The end of March, not long after lambing time began, saw us called out already, but lambing calls can last until around mid-May during some years and so, just when one thinks of lazier days, times can become busy again.

Another call saw us heading into the hills at a place where foxes have caused problems for decades, though this was no sheep farm, just a sort of smallholding where hens, ducks and geese were kept, more or less in a sort of free-range style. The old man had difficulty rounding them all up at night

Rockpiles often hold foxes.

Bella, emerging from the earth at the old quarry.

Logan of the Coniston with a lamb-worrying fox.

Foot packs are often called out to deal with lamb worrying foxes.
(Jim Dalton & the Blencathra, 1920s).

and so quite a number of his livestock went missing on a fairly regular basis, usually during the hours of darkness, though sometimes he was raided during daylight hours too. There is an old quarry nearby and Reynard often took his prize into the piles of rocks to be found there and this is where my terriers and lurchers came into their own.

I had Rock and Ghyll out with me that day and Gary had his lurcher, Tiny, a large running dog, in spite of the name, alongside him, but this was testing ground for any lurcher and my own had failed to catch foxes here, as they followed in the wake of their foe as it led them across the incredibly rough rock and scree-strewn ground. I loosed Rock and, sure enough, Reynard was at home, her strong steady bay telling of the find and the whereabouts of her quarry.

The vixen wasn't for bolting, however, but twenty-minutes of 'persuasion' from my old bitch soon changed her mind and she shot out of the rocks on the far side of the pile, some way from the lurcher as it happened, which is rather a typical scenario where foxes are concerned. They have not become known as cunning creatures for nothing! It is a well-known fact that Reynard, in many instances and especially at rock spots, will craftily look out, sometimes at several different exits, before finally bolting, often choosing one well away from hounds, lurchers, or standing guns. The instinct to survive is incredibly strong in Vulpes vulpes.

Tiny saw his quarry and was off, crossing the obstacle-clad quarry floor at great speed, but without the dexterity Reynard was so cleverly displaying. On more open ground, though, Tiny shortened the distance between them quite considerably, but then our vixen would make for a large pile of boulders and she increased the gap yet more each time they entered rougher terrain. She seemed to glide across the rocky landscape, while the lurcher fumbled awkwardly, but then, when they came to more level and open country once more, the lurcher became graceful and elegant again, now making the fox look a little awkward and uncomfortable.

This went on for some time, but the large crags above saved her, for she climbed these with the agility of a cat and left the lurcher way in the rear. Our vixen saved her brush and sped on, away from the danger, to run another day. However, she had cubs in here and Rock made short work of them in next to no time, emerging when the job was finished. A vixen will often defend her cubs with great venom, though not always. I take no pleasure in killing cubs, but they were the reason for the losses at the nearby farm belonging to Mr Ashworth and those losses promptly ended after our encounter at the

A fit, muscular terrier will catch the Judges eye.

Crag – a good head is one quality Judges should look for on any terrier.

Terriers are allowed to slow down a little during springtime.
(Nuttall's Patterdales).

Brian Nuttall exercising his charges.

Alf Johnston's Oregill 'My Masterpiece'.
Early breeders bred away from open-coated Bedlington types and
began creating the harsh-coated Lakeland.

old quarry. Fox control is not pleasant and I would not even attempt to give the impression that it is, but such means are absolutely vital when a man's livelihood is being threatened and good working terriers play a vital role in effective control of predators.

A couple of ventures at livestock killing foxes had been carried out so far this springtime and I must say my small team were looking a little jaded after a long season and a heavy workload. We would be out after mink soon and I wanted my team to get a little rest before we began, but that was looking more and more unlikely at the moment. It wasn't long, in fact, before we were out again and this time Gary was carrying his gun.

A farmer had been complaining of lamb losses and he believed the culprit was coming out of a deep-cut wooded valley, which I knew to hold a decent-sized fox population, as I had hunted this place on a number of occasions. One of the best hunts was one February day during the previous season when I had three terriers out, these being Ghyll, Rock and Crag. We had drawn up and down the valley and tried every earth and covert within reach, but without any success at all. They had put up a number of rabbits from the sparse undergrowth and had chased them to their lairs, or until lost on top, but foxes were rather elusive to say the least. The arctic winds blew down from the north and every now and then a sprinkling of snow fell on the ground, mingling with the white of the frost that still lay in more shaded and sheltered places, which stung my cheeks and eyes as I watched my team at work.

We must have searched high and low for hours on what should have been a perfect day to find a fox to ground, but still they failed to find and there was only one last place to try; a line of low-hung bushes with undergrowth surrounding them, but I wasn't hopeful, as this covert had never held before. However, the terriers suddenly rushing forward into the undergrowth betrayed the presence of something interesting and, sure enough, the intense baying, more serious and intent than that on rabbit, rang out into the cold air, telling of Reynard's quick exit as they entered his den. He was away and I had a good view of him as he fled across the hillside, skirting a small wood and then disappearing into yet more undergrowth, which was rather dense for the time of year.

Ghyll led as the terriers went off in pursuit, following by scent now that he had gone from sight and eventually finding him again underneath a large stickpile by the side of a small wood. They struggled to find a way in and I coupled Crag and Rock and allowed Ghyll to attempt to reach his foe, which, it has to be said, wasn't for moving again. However, Ghyll managed to push in and now his fox, reluctant to face him, decided to bolt and away he went once again, with the terriers, in their role as hounds at the moment, following eagerly.

Their fox led them over Kirkburn Marsh and into the big woodlands to the north, where, at last, Reynard shook off his pursuers. He was a fine dog fox and would no doubt stamp his type on quite a few litters to come and I was certainly happy for him to escape, for control is not always about killing foxes. Disturbing earths and coverts prevents foxes from 'packing' and this means fewer lambs and chickens are taken and far fewer ground-nesters are caught and killed. Hunting in packs is always easier for foxes, though it is important that they are not allowed to do so.

However, back to our lamb worrying fox. Gary and I tried everywhere we could think of and at last Crag found in a small rockpile in the south of the valley, not far from Kirkburn Marsh where our previous hunt had occurred. He bayed for a while, but then fell silent and it wasn't long before he emerged with a dead cub, about four weeks of age. This was April and the daffodils were out in force, the singing of the birds intense for much of the day and the trees were beginning to bud, the skies much brighter with a slightly warming breeze pushing the broken cloud across the bright blue above. The cubs must have been born some time during March and they were growing well. They were certainly being cared for properly, but one thing was rather strange – there wasn't any sign of a vixen or dog fox anywhere near the place and none barked a warning signal as we stood outside the earth. Crag killed and fetched out of that spot a full litter of cubs and this ended the lamb worrying as far as I am aware, so it was still effective control, but a most unusual event, for I have never seen a litter without at least their mother at that stage of their lives. We buried the cubs next to the earth and moved on, without any feeling of excitement, saddened instead, but knowing that such an outcome would still produce good results for local farmers.

There was maybe another month of lamb worrying calls to come in and undoubtedly some more work for the terriers, though I wasn't having as hard a time as some. One Huntsman I was speaking to, who hunts a foot pack in Wales, had been out on lambing calls for seven days a week since lambing began and he still had plenty of calls coming in!

Spring is not only a time for making oneself available to farmers and shepherds, in case of troublesome foxes, but it is also a time to slow down a little and give the terriers a few rest days whenever possible. It is important to keep your earth dogs fit and active during the season and exercise, as well as work, plays a vital role in this, but now is the time to slacken a little and allow your charges some relaxation time.

Of course, with lambing calls coming in it is vital to keep them in relatively fit condition, so exercise is still important, but a few days off would not go amiss. Also, the showing season begins in early spring and terriers must be in good shape if they are to show themselves well, but it would be good to slow down a little and maybe have shorter exercise periods. If so, then reduce the food a little too. Terriers are allowed to gain a *little* weight during the off-season, but they must remain on the leaner, rather than the fatter, side, though being underweight is definitely out of the question. Underweight terriers should not be given a ticket when being exhibited, for they are being neglected to some extent and the owner, rather than the dog itself, is not worthy of any recognition. That being said, illness, or even a heavy workload, can take weight off a terrier in no time at all, but still, they should not be shown until back up to the correct weight. It is unfair to a good terrier when it is exhibited in poor condition, so keep them out of the ring until fit to be in it. Terriers of the correct weight, looking fit and muscular, or even carrying a *little* too much weight, are the ones that should catch the Judges eye, providing they are of the correct type of course.

Betwixt lambing calls and other springtime duties, such as cleaning out and disinfecting terrier boxes and kennels, as well as cleaning equipment that will not be needed until the new season, and storing it safely, it is also important to prepare your charges for the show season, if you are so inclined. Not everyone enjoys the atmosphere of the show ring and some keep terriers that, whilst working very well, are just not suited to exhibiting. Each to their own and if your terriers suit you and do the job you require of them, then all well and good. Some, however, enjoy to show when not at work and a little effort can go a long way to enjoying more success.

Stripping out a rough coat, for instance, will remove all dead hair and this should be carried out using a stripping knife, which has a serrated edge. By pulling out the dead hair, one allows a new coat to grow and this, if the coat is right in the first place, of course, will grow back harsh and tight and will impress any judge of the right mind. Working qualities are what should be looked for and good coat is essential on a working terrier. True, a poor coat will in no way hinder actual working ability, but it does pose a certain amount of risk to an earth dog. Freezing weather, especially rain and cold winds combined, could easily kill a terrier without a good coat, as could becoming trapped to ground in freezing temperatures and having to spend the night in a cold rockpile. Many earth dogs with poor jackets have perished under such conditions and that is why the early fell-hunters bred away from the open-coated Bedlington type of fell terrier and created the harsh-coated Lakeland instead.

It was during that early spring that I had my first outing of the year at a show and my charges did rather well. The show was in the south of Lancashire, close to the Cheshire border, and I was exhibiting Ghyll and Crag. Ghyll had the slape coat of the Buck/Breay strain, through the dogs of John Parks, but he was rather tidy in stamp, having some of the blood of Gary Middleton's dogs in his breeding. Bruce Hardy had bred him out of his dog Snap, a sensible terrier that could finish foxes without taking too much punishment, and Ghyll had certainly developed into a superb worker of similar abilities to his sire. That day I took the breed championship with Ghyll and also won best Lakeland with Crag, though I was most disappointed at the end of it all when the judge picked out a near pure bull terrier that had half of its face missing and fresh wounds inflicted, no doubt, by rather illegal quarry.

I later discovered that this judge had been keeping working terriers for only a few short years and, because he had won a few venues with his charges, he was being asked to judge. I have seen many veteran terriers of excelling abilities at work with few scars, even in old age. Not that they haven't been bitten on several occasions, well, most of them anyway, but the wounds had covered over with rough facial fur, or they had faded over the years, and little evidence remained, yet they have worked fox regular for several seasons, many alongside hounds. So picking scars is ridiculous. What one must look for are qualities that will aid a terrier at work, such as being spannable and having the correct jacket, as well as a decent sized head and jaws. Crag had a harsh jacket, being of a Lakeland stamp bred out of Middleton's famous strain, with just a dash of Ward blood included too, but it wasn't in the best condition for that show. I hadn't stripped it, just tidied it up, for I had Crag in the Great Yorkshire Show later in the year and stripping his coat now would have meant that it would have 'blown' (lost its best condition) by then. I could understand Crag not winning overall because his coat was not at its best, but still, he was far better than that bull terrier cross which would never have got down a fox earth. Personally, I would have given the championship to a superb Border terrier that won best of breed, but certainly not to that ugly thing he picked out.

May came around and fox cubs were now growing and developing rapidly and they needed more constant food as a consequence, so lambing calls continued. Bradley had lost lambs at an alarming rate and we had searched all over the place. Tim's Lurcher found and marked a rockpile and Tim came for me straight away, but by the time we got there the vixen had cleverly shifted her cubs. Rock and Bella went wild at the earth, going in and out and seeking their quarry under the piles of huge boulders, scent was that fresh, but they had definitely just vacated the premises and the cunning fox had saved her litter. This scenario has occurred on quite a few occasions and no doubt some readers will be familiar with such circumstances.

These May-days were rather warm affairs and the situation wasn't helped by the fact that we were hunting hilly country, with quite a large amount of moorland, rock and scree to contend with. The weather was dry and rather sultry and it was hard work wandering all over the place and checking every likely spot and it wasn't until we had exhausted most of the grounds that we finally found a litter. Again, though, no vixen or dog fox was anywhere near the place and a litter, quite a well-grown one at that, was found. These may have been the ones that had been moved earlier, I do not know, though I think it unlikely, as it wasn't too far from the original spot and a cunning vixen will usually take her litter for quite some distance when disturbed. Rock and Bella now entered the large rockpile and the lurcher stood guard. If any bolted, then the dog had a good chance of running them down, though one can never guarantee a successful catch.

The two terriers worked the pile superbly and quickly found, baying and scratching at the hard rock in an attempt to reach their quarry, which was skulking out of reach. Because the cubs were smaller and much more slender than the terriers, they could squeeze themselves into spaces where a rabbit would have difficulty getting, and so the two earth dogs found it impossible to get up to their foe. In fact, their claws were bleeding at the end of it, they had dug that hard at the unyielding rock.

Tim and I began to dig down to them as best we could, in an attempt to clear a way for them, but it was to no avail. We dug for three hours and more and still we couldn't open up a way to our quarry. In the end we knew we were beaten and had to give this litter best, knowing that at least the vixen would now move them on and this may have helped curb the lamb worrying, though I was doubtful.

Apart from a large badger sett at another rock spot, there were no other places to try around the farm and the terriers had proven of limited use in this instance, and so Tim lamped the fields during the hours of darkness instead, shooting two foxes, which then ended Bradley's troubles. It wasn't the end I had wanted, but never mind, for there are times, sometimes many, when you just cannot get a fox, even with good terriers and lurchers at your disposal, and in such circumstances it is best to relent and try other methods, for a farmer cannot be left to suffer predation of his livestock. As I write this, I know of a chap who has lost eighteen of his chickens to a fox and I will try to sort out the matter as quickly as possible. It is not my hunting ground, but I know a couple of lads who cover that area and they will have a good idea where it is coming from and will no doubt deal with this problem fox.

Just one more outing was on the cards for that year and a good hard dig would at last end the season for me. Again, lambing troubles had us out and about on another warm May morning and Crag and Rock were out that day, coupled together, or loose when hunting any undergrowth dense enough to hold a fox. We searched high and low and again found at another rockpile, though our quarry wasn't too deep and Crag, after quickly finding, could reach his quarry and he bottled it up in a tight spot. Tim and I dug down, shifting large amounts of rock, both large and small, as well as shale and loose clay, while Crag bayed like crazy at his fox. He was not a hard dog and would never have killed any larger than a September cub (foxes have reached adulthood by this time, though they have yet to fill out and put on muscle), but he was a superb terrier for digging to and would stick close to his foe and keep it busy until reached. I enjoyed some good digs with him and he sometimes rushed in and seized the quarry by the cheek, thus securing it, when I broke through and had cleared a bit of a space in order to make room to manoeuvre.

Rockpiles are always challenging territory when it comes to digging and one must take care not to loose rocks that are acting as supports, for then a rush in of soil and of stone would seriously threaten the welfare of your terrier. Thankfully though, and rather unusually, our quarry hadn't gone in too deep and so after some time we eventually broke through and Crag had stayed with a small vixen until we managed to reach and get him out. It had been a very successful dig and a good result for us, as well as for the local farmers.

We had enjoyed some superb hunting and terrier work throughout that season and the lambing calls had produced a most satisfactory end to the season, but it was now time to allow less troublesome foxes to breed and replenish their numbers, which means strictly leaving them alone whenever possible, until the new season begins. The small team of terriers had worked

Steve Dawes, terrierman for Coniston foxhounds,
finds spring a busy time dealing
with lamb-worrying foxes.

Hardisty's Turk

hard, but now it was time to allow them some rest for a couple of weeks, giving them a little less food and only light exercise, until it was time to get among the riverbanks again in search of one of Britain's worst of alien predators – the mink.

Springtime for professional hunt terriermen is also a busy time. Some packs operate a call-out system during this charming and delightful season and often hounds will hunt a lamb-worrying fox well into May, with terriers being used to account for those that go to ground, as no earth stopping is practised at this time of the year, for the aim is to account for a fox, not hunt it. And so hounds and terriers can be out for several days in a week in some countries and often gamekeepers will benefit from such provisions too. Once the shooting season ends, more time can be devoted to fox control and springtime can be busy periods for all who hunt over keepered land. A gamekeeper, for sure, will not allow any onto their land who do not carry out effective control, as they will soon have young game birds being reared in the woods and out on the pastures, so it is vital to keep the fox population in check and they definitely will not tolerate foxes breeding on their beat.

Rats are another problem for gamekeepers and late winter, early spring, is also a good time for tackling these wily rodents and a good team of terriers, with ferrets and smoking machines being used for bolting purposes, will make a massive dent in the rat population in no time at all, provided one is diligent and much time is spent at this pursuit. It was during the latter half of May, when my terriers were just enjoying some rest, that a call came in from a local stables that was having problems with rats. There wasn't a huge population, but still, the owners were not happy in the knowledge of 'ratty' running around all over the place and nibbling away at valuable feed stocks, and so I was happy to help out and was soon at the yard, on that very morning I received the telephone call, in order to deal with the problem.

I took Crag and Rock along and both had experience of tackling this hard-bitten creature. Rock had taken part in some mammoth ratting sessions and she had proven true at marking and incredibly adept at taking such quarry. Crag had taken a few rats around Gary Middleton's farm before I bought him and so he would be useful to have around. Just a couple of terriers is enough in this situation, when one is on only limited ground and there are fierce kicking horses around every corner. Safety is of paramount importance when ratting and especially around farmyards and stables where there are many obstacles. If 'ratty' chose to run into a small space where a horse was tethered and the terrier got in too, then your dog could so easily be trampled.

Terriers ratting.

Some horses are wicked beggars and will do their utmost to stamp on a small dog, so make certain stable doors are shut and your terrier cannot get in. If rats do get into such places, then they are best left, or chased out of there by someone with experience of working with horses, if they have enough 'bottle' to do so of course!

Rock and Crag were soon marking at a freshly dug spot and the runs indicated regular use. I put in a ferret and shortly afterwards a large rat was on the move, shooting out of the burrow and heading for a grassy bank, but Rock had it and a crushing bite, combined with a violent shake, soon 'fettled it'. Another was out and Crag was in hot pursuit as it ran among the chickens, which had gathered round, curious as to what we were doing, but he was not the brightest of dogs and, once the rat had popped into a drain and escaped, disappearing from view as quickly as it had bolted from its lair, he was soon going, instead, after a rather bemused and hysterical chicken and this brought a rather rapid and severe reprimand from myself. A well-grown youngster, complete with gangly legs, known as a 'grey' in country circles, now erupted from that hole and it used every obstacle to get away, but Crag had it at the drain, before it could follow in the wake of the former rat. My ferret, Titch, was soon at the exit and she was picked up without any problems. Ferrets can be shy when emerging, popping back in and out of reach whenever the owner approaches, but if one doesn't rush about and you allow it to come out and have a sniff around for a few seconds, before gently reaching down and picking it up, then this shyness, which can be rather irritating, can be avoided. Plenty of handling when they are kits can also help avoid this problem.

No more rats were at home at this spot and so we moved on, with the dogs casting all over the place, around the chicken house especially, with the flourishing pastures and leafy woodlands as our backdrop. 'The darling buds of May' had truly blossomed by this time and the heat of the sun and the air full of birdsong made it a delight to be out and about. The trouble was, the grass was also growing at a rapid rate and some of the rat holes were hard to find as the terriers marked at a steep bank. In went my ferret and out popped 'ratty', from an undiscovered exit hole somewhere among the undergrowth, but Crag knew it was afoot and he had it soon after. It was a 'big 'un', but the terrier soon rid the stable owner of yet another pest. Another was out, but this one escaped into a nearby drain that was unworkable and so it had to be left.

The terriers now marked at a hole with a slight trickle of water coming

A rat is accounted for.

A large rat taken with the terriers.

from it and I tried the ferret, but she wouldn't go. No doubt the lair was sopping wet inside, for I have worked wet drains for rabbits on several occasions with my ferrets, so this must have been unusually wet. Titch would go in a little, but would quickly turn around and emerge. And so we were forced to leave this place well alone, though I suspected a rat had slunk away unseen from the lair we had just worked and had popped in here, no doubt considering it a safer refuge. Ferrets are game creatures indeed, but certain situations will prevent them from carrying out their vocation. Wet drains are one such problem, especially if there is lots of water inside, while doe rats with young are another problem. Many think that a ferret is a coward if it will not face a doe rat with young, or when birth is imminent, for a rat will not leave a nest it has prepared for the arrival of its family, despite it being empty. Some ferrets will tackle a doe rat and kill it and I have owned such ones myself, for a rat, no matter how big, cannot match the armour of a polecat, which is basically what a ferret is. Others will lunge at rats and then dodge the retaliation, or dig around the nest looking for an advantage, while others will simply turn around and emerge if 'ratty' stands its ground, but this cannot ever be considered as cowardice.

Ferrets retain the wild instincts of their ancestors, polecats, and so try to avoid injury. When injured a wild animal is likely to die of either infection, or starvation, as it will be incapable of catching prey. That is why sick, or injured, foxes will often take to raiding farmyards and killing lambs, simply because they cannot catch wild game. So do not consider any ferret a coward, as it is simply using such instinct to avoid injury. I have owned ferrets that, once bitten by a rat, will not face them in battle, but are still capable of bolting these rodents. Many rats, most in fact, will bolt at the mere scent of a ferret, so one that will not tackle a doe with young can still be most useful. If, however, a ferret will not even enter a lair smelling of rat, then it is best used on rabbits alone.

Our morning ended and a few rats had perished, while one or two had escaped. Still, we had had a productive time and the sparse population had been severely dented, which showed when I next visited the place and could find none. I am sure there were still one or two around, but not in any significant numbers. Sometimes one must shift hordes of rats to sort out a problem, while at other times one must remove only a few, if the population is caught early enough, before breeding has swelled numbers to any degree. Keepered spots are probably the best for finding large numbers, as rats feed on the grain put down for pheasants and the large supply means large numbers of litters being born during the warmer months, though rats will breed almost all year round if winter proves mainly mild. And so, once the shooting season has ended and one can get in among the rats, often vast numbers are encountered and it is hard work for both dogs and masters tackling them. Smoking machines are very useful in such a situation, as large numbers will produce several doe rats with young, which presents a problem for ferrets, though ferrets can be utilized too. Also, digging at the earths, especially shallow ones out in the field and among the woodland floor, is also an effective way of flushing these rodents out from their burrows.

Soon after my visits to the stables I was out exercising my charges when they picked up a scent at a small fishing pond nearby. At first I thought they were on a mink, but shortly afterwards a large rat was running around among the undergrowth, with the small pack in close and rather hot pursuit. Had this been winter time and the grasses flattened, beaten down by the wind, rain, hail and snow, then they would surely have nailed it within seconds, but as it was it kept ahead of them by using every place of concealment to great effect. It is surprising the distances rats will cover when being hunted and the pack worked the bank right along the pond, before dropping down to the dyke below and hunting along here with great excitement and urgency. The terriers competed for the lead place and each took their turn as they hunted it for quite some distance, before it finally eluded capture by sneaking into a drain which took away the waters running down this dyke. It had been a cracking hunt, but the odds were definitely in favour of 'ratty' as it secured that creepy scaly tail, holding onto it for another day.

This was meant to be a rest period 'twixt controlling fox numbers and then that of mink, but the terriers were putting in quite a bit of work among the rats that springtime and another cracking hunt took place shortly afterwards. I was at yet another popular fishing lodge when the terriers again began hunting around, having caught the scent of something interesting, which, as with the previous outing, was skulking below the undergrowth. The terriers suddenly moved up a couple of gears and rushed forward, their sterns wagging furiously, their noses constantly testing the scent wafting to them through the dense tangle of grasses.

Terriers have great drive when they are on a fresh scent and into the undergrowth they went, pushing through it, despite brambles and thorns of all kinds, eventually forcing their rat out of cover and into the open. A large rat emerged and crossed the footpath, before running down the steep bank and plopping into the water, sending ever-widening ripples across the

Future stock.

glassy surface reflecting the broken-blue of the sky above, the tops of the trees which were now almost in full leaf, the birds singing for their very lives from the lush branches. Crag, Ghyll and Rock hunted superbly, having never seen the rat up until this time and thus hunting by scent alone. All were absolutely true to the line as they rushed forward to the water, casting their noses across the surface in an effort to grasp which way their quarry had headed. The rat was making for the far bank and I quickly holloa'd on the pack, which ran ahead of me with great eagerness indeed, looking for their foe at all times, their noses still twitching as they tested the air for scent.

As we made for the bank where 'ratty' was about to emerge from the water, he turned around and headed off elsewhere and that is the way things went for quite a while. The rat wouldn't come out of the water, but it couldn't stay in there indefinitely and eventually made it onto dry land ahead of us, rushing up the bank and disappearing into the undergrowth, with the eager pack not far behind. They hit off the line once more and followed it into the long grasses and brambles, going down the steep hillside and to the brook below. They took up the scent and followed it along the bank and then dropped into the water's edge, scrambling now to the twisted mass of tree roots by the bank and marking with great eagerness indeed. I was soon on the spot and attempted to dig on, while the terriers all played a part in the proceedings, but the roots were just too well established and we were getting nowhere fast. It had been a superb hunt and they almost had it, but that rat saved its tail and lived to be hunted another day.

Springtime wore relentlessly on and the bare landscape of winter was now lush and flourishing and the birds were busy rearing their fast-growing fledglings. The lambs were now too big for foxes to bother them, in the main, though one or two may still have been taken, even as late as August, or even September. I have found large lambs killed by foxes at this time of year and the throat is always pierced through by those deadly fangs, where Reynard has throttled his kill. But, mostly, the growing, bleating 'woolly backs' could now graze in relative peace and fatten themselves in readiness of the autumn sheep sales.

Ratting was now more or less out of the question, at most venues anyway, as the undergrowth made finding holes, runs, and the bolting rats themselves, almost impossible. Whenever a rat was on the loose at such places the terriers, although they hunted extremely keenly and did their utmost, just found it impossible to get on terms with their quarry. Also, if a ferret is to ground at such a location, then seeing it emerge can be utterly impossible

Summer is a time for breeding new stock.

Spring & summer is a time to enjoy country shows.

and one can travel a surprising distance when unseen and it may be lost. And so our attentions now turned to the local mink population, which was always a problem. A chap who had an allotment had recently had sixteen of his chickens killed by a mink, which was coming from the very brook where 'ratty' had just escaped the attentions of my small pack of earth dogs.

Although the professional terrierman at several packs up and down the country will make himself available for lamb worrying calls during the spring months, from the time lambing begins, usually in late March, to around the middle of May, he will also be busy with other jobs that are linked to hunting. For instance, hunt Jumps, gates and fences may need some attention and these he will repair, or even replace, where necessary. His terriers may well have had a busy season, but now they enjoy a less busy time, unless, that is, he works them with a local pack of mink-hounds, if demands on his time allow.

Those who have keepered land in their hunt country will also make themselves available to aid gamekeepers with pest control, whether it be rats, or problem foxes, from the end of the shooting season, until young poults are put down in the woods. And so spring can be incredibly busy for the professional terrierman. Summer may bring a little light relief, in that no more lambing calls are necessary, but still, repairs to furnishings throughout the hunt country, as well as aiding the kennelman with fallen livestock collections, will continue unabated. And, of course, his terriers will continue to need good care and attention, as well as a certain amount of exercise. Terriers easily become bored and frustrated when not kept active enough, though cutting down on feed a little while less activity is the norm', may help. Spring and summer is also a time to enjoy country shows and to breed new stock when youngsters are needed as veterans near retiring age. As springtime merges into early summer, the terriers generally enjoy a little lighter workload and they can then begin to recuperate in readiness of the season to come.

It has been a busy time for the professional terrierman too, and especially for the fell pack Huntsman and Whip as they answer lambing calls from their local farmers, usually from late March or early April, until around the middle of May when these calls often stop coming in. It is now time to carry out necessary work at the kennels, such as repainting, as well as to take hounds and terriers back to their places of 'walk'. Local farmers and villagers are usually the ones who walk hounds for the Lake District packs and they have the same hound or terrier returned to them each summer. Far less terriers are put out at walk than used to be the case, and it can be difficult finding walks for all the hounds due to modern life, with many followers coming from built-up areas where it isn't possible to walk hounds, but still the fell packs soldier on and this ancient traditional way of life remains an important part of Cumbrian culture. By the end of May the repairs and painting jobs will have been carried out and now the Huntsman and Whip are forced to find work for the summer months, until hunting begins again in September.

Middleton's old Rex, son of Wilk's Rock.

Summer

The bluebells had put on a terrific display this year and I enjoyed exercising my charges among woodlands covered in them. The trees were not yet in full leaf through May and the early part of June and the sun-dappled woodland floor, covered in the delicate hue of the bluebells, had been a delight to walk amongst. But now the bluebells were far past their best and the trees were at last in full green leaf, with less sunlight reaching the woodland floor.

My terriers had enjoyed a couple of weeks of rest and light exercise after some fairly hectic ratting sessions, once the lambing calls had finished, but now it was time to get out on the local rivers and reservoirs in search of mink. However, with the lambing calls over, it was time for me to do some of my own repairs back at home and the kennels were thoroughly inspected for rot, or holes in the mesh of the run. Also, the chill of winter, often still felt during the springtime, was now long gone and the air had warmed considerably, so it was time to give the kennels a thorough disinfecting. This is vital if one is to keep the terriers in tip-top condition.

My kennel for two had an inside area of six feet in length and three feet in width, while the outside run was six by six. This gave them plenty of room and, if one provides regular exercise, was, I suppose, unnecessarily large, for two terriers could easily manage in less space. I provided an enclosed box of around two by two feet and had newspaper inside for bedding. This does not allow place for fleas to breed and is easily and very cheaply disposed of and replaced. The inside run had either newspaper or sawdust on the floor, to dry up urine, but the run was bare concrete, which is easily cleaned. A bowl of fresh water was provided, which was accessible at all times.

I emptied the bedding box and disposed of the old newspaper. I had put a mixture of disinfectant and warm water into a spray gun and generously covered both outside and inside of the box with the mixture, until it was well soaked. Wait for a sunny day to carry out such thorough cleaning, as time must be allowed for the box and kennel to dry, *before* putting the occupants back.

I sprayed and mopped the inside of the kennel and made certain that the interior received a generous covering, even into the corners and cracks

An outside run with plenty of room for 2 terriers.

Kennels need regular and thorough cleaning.

where deadly germs may linger and fester. The food and water bowls also received a good cleaning and now it was time to turn my attention to the run. The mesh and wood panelling was soaked in the spray and the hose-pipe turned on the concrete until any muck was washed away. I then filled a bucket with hot water and disinfectant and emptied it onto the concrete, before scrubbing thoroughly with a yard brush. This took off any stains, or debris left from droppings and urine and the kennel fairly sparkled after this diligent treatment.

Two thorough disinfectants per year are necessary; one at the beginning of summer and again just before the autumn, while good cleaning practise must be carried out week in, week out, throughout the year, though a lighter disinfectant of the run and kennel once a week will suffice during the winter and early spring, with such measures taking place more often when warmer weather prevails. During summer I mopped the kennel and washed out the run every single day without fail, in order to keep flies and odours at bay, not to mention possible infections.

I had taken Rock with me when I got married and left home, while Bella was left with my mother, as she was her 'favourite', though I continued to work her whenever possible. Rock was a housedog and she, alongside Ghyll, was kept indoors, while Crag was out in the kennel. This meant I had some space and so I contacted Gary Middleton and he agreed to loan me a young black and tan Lakeland bitch called Judy. She hadn't seen any work, but I was sure she would come in handy whilst hunting mink. She was twelve months of age and just right for starting, so I was keen to get out among the waterways. Our first foray was at a large reservoir where mink had been killing a smallholder's livestock. I would draw the edges of this large body of water, but it had many tributaries; small wooded brooks lined with brambles and bracken, which was ideal territory for this ruthless and rather evasive predator.

I had a small pack out that day, with four and a half couple of terriers milling around busily searching for scent, and it wasn't long before they began speaking to a line amongst the briars above a narrow brook. I was sure they were on a mink, as scent took them all over the place and it was obvious that they were now in pursuit of their quarry, eagerly rushing along the banks of the stream and heading towards a drain which led under the old and now disused railway cutting.

They were as keen as mustard and they fairly flew through the undergrowth, before finally dropping into the brook itself and heading back towards the reservoir, going now at an even faster pace. I scanned the pebbly depths for the dark form of a fleeing mink, but instead I caught sight of one of the largest rats I have ever seen; fat, massive, its huge bulk ambling towards the large body of water with the pack of eager hunters bearing down rapidly upon it. At the very last minute, it swam under the water and simply disappeared. Sometimes a hunted animal, when startled, can suddenly cease giving off scent and I can only assume that that is what happened in this instance, for they could make nothing of it after that and we were forced to move on.

We failed to find a mink, despite searching everywhere, the terriers casting at every likely place, even the banks of the nearby river, but I did meet up with a chap who could shed some light on why our quarry was more than a little elusive. A friend of his owned a terrier and it had caught and killed two mink while out at exercise, so it seemed the problem was solved, for the moment anyway. So the next venue would be further north and hopefully we would find this time.

It was a warm sunny morning with a clear blue sky and I was eager to get onto the river in search of mink, for this quarry is challenging to catch, but it is also rather an expert hunter that will readily kill bank voles, moorhens, coot, ducks, young geese (as well as adults if hungry enough) kingfishers, sandmartins, dippers, farmed chickens and anything else it can get its teeth into. So one is doing both the farming community, as well as local wildlife, a favour when one rids the waterways of such an animal.

Judy had shown little interest on her first hunt, though she had got her nose down at times, but this morning she showed an eager and willing spirit as we drew along the banks of the river. We covered quite an area and found the easily defined footprints of our elusive prey at soft sandy spots. I had taken quite a number of rats from this place in years gone by, but the mink had quickly seen them off and rats were now rather conspicuous by their absence. This may have seemed like a good thing, but the trouble was bank voles had disappeared with equal rapidity too. Also, the sandmartins no longer came to nest on the exposed sandy banks, when previously they nested there during every spring without fail.

After trying all kinds of different places without success, Rock showed interest at a stickpile and it wasn't long before Judy joined her, keenly marking at the spot with tails wagging furiously. All of the terriers converged on the spot and soon afterwards they were all yapping and wailing and attempting to dig through to their foe, which they knew was lurking somewhere beneath the almost impenetrable tangle of branches and washed up debris.

Rock managed to push herself in and soon afterwards her quarry decided it was best to get out of there, and rather swiftly. It left its former refuge unseen, but the terriers beginning to cast all around told me that it had indeed bolted and I knew this time that they were definitely hunting a mink. Rock hit off the line first and the rest of the pack quickly followed, hunting right along the riverbank for quite some distance and leaving their master far in the rear. It was far too warm by now to be a good scenting day and, once the mink had got among dense undergrowth, they struggled to follow and eventually lost the animal far downstream. It had been a good and exciting hunt, however, though I had hoped to account for this quarry as quickly as possible. Mink, though, are incredibly difficult to catch as they can get into places that are impossible to dig, so a combination of hunting them with dogs and trapping them is best used in many areas where mink typically get among deep places that cannot be dug. This was during the 1990s when hunting with dogs in England, Wales and Scotland enjoyed no restrictions at all and using a pack of terriers was incredibly effective and exciting. Even now, a pack can be used to locate and flush mink and foxes in Scotland, while in England and Wales two dogs can be used to locate and flush such animals, though they must be despatched using a suitable gun. I found no more mink that day and it would be a couple of weeks later when I was out again.

I had been to one or two more shows during that late spring and early summer and had done okay, winning veterans with Rock, who wasn't a particularly good show dog, and taking prizes with Crag and Ghyll. Bella was very much like an old fashioned Bedlington and some said she was similar to the old strains of Irish Wheaten (which, I believe, showed some Bedlington influence), so she was in no way suitable for a show ring and was never touched by a judge's hands. However, Crag wasn't at his best just yet. I had tidied up his coat a little, but he needed stripping in time for the Great Yorkshire Show in July.

Early summer would be a little too late, so at the back end of spring I decided to take out his old jacket so that the new could grow just in time for this prestigious event. I put him on a bench at a suitable height and covered him with chalk. This takes off the oil in the fur and allows one a better grip.

Taking the stripping knife, I grabbed the fur 'twixt the serrated edge and thumb and pulled out all of the dead hair, with Crag facing away from me as I pulled his fur in the direction in which it grows. This was done all over his body and on his head, particularly around the ears, as well as on his front

In Scotland a terrier pack can be used to flush to guns.

Stickpiles hold a variety of quarry, including mink.

I had taken a few prizes at shows by early summer.

Rock being Judged at the Wensleydale Foxhounds Show at Hawes.

and underneath. Then it was time to strip the legs and this can be a time consuming operation, though Wendy, Maurice Bell's daughter, uses electric clippers for doing the legs and underneath and this way it is much quicker, though one gets harder fur growing back when stripping all over. I took out his jacket right down to his undercoat; a lighter coloured, softer fur, and then awaited the new jacket growing through. When it did, Crag had a coat that was harsh, tightly knit and wind and waterproof – just what is needed on a Lakeland terrier. He was a neat little red dog with good bone, plenty of head and jaw, but with a narrow front. He had been fully tested both above and below ground and had proven a very useful worker. I have had better, true, but still, for digging one would have to go a long way to improve on this terrier, as he could both find and stay with his quarry. However, if a fox wouldn't bolt and it could not be dug, then he was not the dog to be to ground in this instance, for, though he worked his fox hard, he wouldn't go in for the kill and a harder terrier, such as Ghyll, was then needed.

Although Lakeland terriers have been bred to be narrow in the shoulders, spannable in the chest and small enough to get to ground, they have also traditionally been bred to have good bone structure. I have seen quite a few smart Lakeland terriers of more recent years that have been too narrow and too light in bone. These weigh very little when picked up and I would not have such a terrier in my kennel, nor would I place one at a show, for they simply do not have enough substance that will enable them to stand their ground against a big hill fox and such terriers are easily 'bossed' by their quarry, looking as though they would blow away in a strong wind. I like substance in my earth dogs and they must have a bit of weight behind them when picked up, while still being small and narrow enough to get to ground.

My bitch Rock, for instance, was around the eighteen-pound mark when at a good working weight. She had good bone and could stand against any fox. Her best quality was her ability to find and her worst was that she lacked a little in the sense department and often took unnecessary punishment, though her stubbornness to refuse to give an inch meant that she often bolted foxes that others couldn't shift – a priceless attribute in a rock-laden country. She had a special knack of working in rock, though I also dug quite a number of foxes with her out of dug-out rabbit holes over the years. She could also work old mineshafts without getting into trouble and she bolted several from such places, though as I got older I did my best to avoid such potential death traps. The only time Rock got into shafts after that was when

Is it a bird?
Is it a plane?
No it's the champion of the terrier show!

she had put a fox out of covert and had then followed it by scent to where it had gone to ground, which happened on quite a few occasions. She was capable of finishing an immature fox during its first year, but after that a wiser, more experienced fox could keep her at bay. A throat hold is what proves fatal to most foxes and if they can keep a terrier from getting such a hold then they will often survive even a long and gruelling dig, though, of course, some are so hard and determined that no fox can live with them.

She was bred by Dave Jones of Urmston, out of Turk and Sally, and she had quite a bit of border in her bloodlines, as well as Buck/Breay bred stock. In fact, when mated to Chris Rainford's Snap, who must also have had quite a bit of this breeding in his pedigree, she produced several Patterdale type fell terriers, with one being a replica of Buck's Black Davy. This dog went to Oldham and spent his life working the South Pennine Mountains, which lie to the east of Manchester.

This breeding has been tried and tested and Bella, one of Rock's pups, literally self-entered from the very first day she was taken out, working like a veteran from day one. Most terriers develop as their entering progresses, but some have such a strong working instinct that they take to their work immediately. The penny drops, so to speak, as soon as they are taken into a working environment. The same thing can happen with lurchers and ferrets, though, obviously, improvements are made with experience.

Judy, the Middleton bred bitch, had showed little interest on her first outing, but during her second trip she had worked very well indeed and I was out again on the water, with Rock and Judy drawing the riverbank. We were deep in a wooded valley surrounded on all sides by high moorland stretching into the near cloudless sky for almost a thousand feet, the green of the bilberry and the brown of the heather standing out starkly far above. The birdsong filled the warm air and damsel flies flitted about in every direction. The growth all around was lush and green and young birds could be heard at their nests as the parent birds visited with food time and again. Part of hunting is to enjoy one's surroundings and I always take time to stand and stare and drink in the whole scene, which, on a lovely summer's day, was enchanting, but I was brought out of my musings by the terriers pushing 'forrard' on a good scent.

I had spoken to a fisherman earlier and he had seen a mink just recently, so I was certain one must be around somewhere; maybe a female with youngsters. I tried my best to keep up, but it was some time before I came upon the two dogs as they followed their scent up the bank and to a large

Dave Jones' Turk, sire of Rock.

Dave Jones' Sally, dam of Rock.

The Pennine mountains have long been hunted using hounds and terriers.
(The Colne Valley Harriers, early 1900s.)

Rock & Snap bred Buck/Breay type offspring.
Two blacks belonging to Steve Robertson.

A typey Lakeland of good substance.
(Steve Robertson's bitch.)

rockpile nearby. They cast everywhere and eventually settled, popping their heads into the many crevices and marking with great excitement. Terriers get more and more wound up as they mark, their frustration growing by the second, especially when they claw at unyielding rocks that just won't give in any way whatsoever. They are not too bad if they can dig in, nearing their quarry, but the rocks weren't going anywhere and I knew our only chance was to attempt to get the mink to bolt. I dug out the smaller rocks and made as much noise as possible, pushing my stick into every hole and shaking it about, while the terriers yapped and whined and made all kinds of noises that I couldn't possibly compete with, until, in the end, I had to give it up as a bad job. At one point the mink actually came to a hole and popped its head out, spitting defiance at the two terriers, before disappearing again, though its ranting and raving could be heard below. Also, the faint squeaking of a young family could also be heard and I knew then that I had no chance of bolting her, for she would remain with her babies no matter what. Frustrated, I called the dogs off and we went in search of another, but without success. As I stated earlier, hunting mink is very challenging indeed and they are difficult to catch, due to their small and slender size, as they can get into places from where it is impossible to shift them.

At last the Great Yorkshire Show came around and my wife and I were away early, in order to attempt to avoid the worst of the traffic, but we still ended up in a jam as we approached Harrogate. Once there I got the terriers ready by cleaning any muck out of their eyes and pulling bits of dead hair from their coats using the serrated edge of the stripping knife, which I simply combed through their jackets. This not only took out dead and poor coloured hair, but it also helped spread the natural oils in the fur and this added to a general appearance of soundness. The hard work they had accomplished throughout the season, the springtime, and now on mink hunting forays, meant they were in superb shape and were well muscled and lean, but without looking neglected and underweight. In fact, they had put a little weight on since the end of the season and it suited them.

I entered the ring confidently, but got nothing with Ghyll, despite the fact that he was already a show champion. Crag was pulled out from a very large Lakeland class and was one of the remaining eight, which the judge had selected. I hoped for at least a rosette and Crag was certainly in good shape, showing himself well, but the others were also a typey bunch and I knew that personal taste would now come into play. The winners would be of a type that the judge would like to have in his kennel. Although he obviously found Crag appealing, he didn't give him a rosette and I was a little disappointed as I exited the show ring. Never mind though. Exhibiting was a way of getting together with like-minded folk and I didn't mind being beaten by worthy opponents. It was when a terrier was put up ahead of mine that just wasn't typey, downright ugly in some cases, which made it a bitter pill to swallow. Those six were among some of the best in the country and I took it on the chin, knowing that just to be picked out at this venue was an achievement in itself. I had done very well with Crag at other shows, often winning best of breed, and continued to do so throughout that summer, but still, I would have liked to have picked up a rosette at the Great Yorkshire Show!

The professional terrierman continues to be busy helping maintain a hunt country and often helping out at the kennels during the summer months and this is the time when he must take his holidays, before the season begins again, though some will spend their leisure time with a pack of mink-hounds, rather than chase the sun abroad. Some will have been busy attending shows, but in June preparations already begin for the season to come and hound exercise is now the main focus. Of course, hound exercise occurs all year round, but during the season it is light and there just to keep hounds happy on days when they are not hunting. Spring and early summer see light exercise too, but then, around the end of June, many packs will begin walking out with hounds in earnest.

At first they will usually ride bicycles in order to take hounds along roads etc, but then they will use horses as the exercise periods lengthen. This is carried out during the early mornings when traffic is nigh on non-existent and the young hounds learn much from such activity. They encounter other dogs, cats and wildlife that is out of bounds to them and this teaches them not to 'riot', that is, chase and hunt quarry they are not entitled to. They also learn to be observant, knowing where their Huntsman is at all times. And the young entry learn much from their elder peers. Hounds should be well mannered and it is the veterans that teach such qualities. A steady older hound is a priceless part of any pack of hounds.

As the summer progresses, so do the exercise periods, lengthening until several miles are covered every morning (though they may be given a rest day or two each week) and hounds become well muscled and hard in the pad. Pads can become badly torn during hunting days and hardening them with plenty of roadwork is essential. The spring has seen a little less discipline in their routine, but now they build up that discipline until

Crag after winning best of breed.

Steve Robertson winning the Scottish Championships with Fell.

Shows are enjoyable during the off-season,
though it is good to win.

Hounds enjoying summer's rest. Pre-season exercise begins in late June.

Terriers need exercise to keep them fit and happy. Nuttall's Buster enjoying a run.

Pads need hardening and exercise on roads will accomplish this,
ready for when work begins again.

autumn hunting begins in August or September, though one pack I know of sometimes starts at the end of July, which, in my opinion, is a little too early. Exercise periods also do the hounds good both mentally and emotionally. Bored hounds, bored dogs in general, can become a problem, being difficult, even impossible, to control, and sheep worrying and cat killing may result, so hounds must be kept happy with good exercise periods, and the same rule applies to terriers.

With the Great Yorkshire Show now over with, it was almost time to begin my own pre-season exercise programme, despite the fact that my bunch were in 'fine fettle' already. Routine is important, however, so I would go through the motions, even though they were fit from their ratting and mink hunting trips. Having said that, whilst hunting the riverbanks and reservoirs, my small pack didn't cover as much ground as they did when hunting the wily fox, so I felt that pre-season exercise was still an important part of my summer activity.

Mid-July is the time I begin pre-season exercise and I increase the distance as the time for hunting again approaches, making certain they are fit enough to cope with the demands of a long day out in the countryside, and, more especially, a long stint to ground. Like Huntsmen, I make certain that my charges get quite a bit of roadwork too and for exactly the same reasons; in order to harden the pads for when they are working under brambles or gorse, the hard surface hopefully not allowing the thorns to penetrate, and for when they were amongst the rocks, as well as to build muscle. Of course, with work and family commitments it is sometimes difficult to give them enough time out each day, so I make up for any shortfalls during days when I have the time to do so. I do not allow the weather to put me off either and use a large umbrella for rainy days, or waterproofs if it is too windy to allow the use of a 'brolly'.

I continued to pay visits to local waterways throughout that summer and Judy began working superbly and was marking accurately and going to ground by the time she was returned to Gary, as there were quite a few drains near to the river and she explored those that had scent inside, either of fox, or mink. True, she hadn't yet seen a fox, but she was well and truly entered to mink. Some of these places were previously unknown to me and future outings would see my terriers bolting foxes from one or two of these earths. Pre-season exercise had been carried out for well over a month by now and at last the time to begin looking for foxes came around once more. Rock was by now getting towards the end of her career, but Crag was in his

They found a few drains while working the rivers.

Shows had been enjoyable
during the off-season.
(Steve Roberts)

(Barry Wild)

Neil Wilson with his minkhunting terriers.

Locating mink with terriers and trapping them is an effective form of control.

The end of summer means hunting time …

… is back again.

Glynis Frain enjoying a summer show.

Judging terriers.

(ph. Neil Wilson)
Neil Wilson's terriers with a mink.

The Kendal & District Otterhounds.
Most packs turned to minkhunting when otterhunting finished.

prime. Bella, though not young, still had plenty of work in her and Ghyll had now served his apprenticeship and was shaping up very well. The coming season looked promising indeed.

Fox marked to ground by Blencathra F.H., hunted by Johnny Richardson.

Autumn

During August, before the season actually begins, it is important to make certain that all of the necessary equipment you will need is in good order. I clean my boots and give them a thorough polish and waxing, ensuring they are waterproof, for there is nothing worse than wet feet for discomfort, especially on a cold day. I use an old pair of boots for hunting along the rivers, as trainers are just too slippery on the bed of stones, but my best are always saved for the season proper.

Leads, couples and collars are all checked and replaced if necessary and digging tackle is cleaned off in readiness of use. I will often keep digging equipment in the boot of my car, lest it is needed, for the ramblers and dog walkers I almost always encounter sometimes get the wrong idea and believe I am out after badgers. Some are reasonable enough to ask and they will accept my explanation that I am controlling fox numbers for the local landowners and farmers, while others are so unreasonable that they will call the police, or follow you round at a distance watching your every move. So I rarely, if ever, carry digging tackle and will go back to the car for it, or usually to the nearest farm, whenever it is needed. I know many of the farmers in my area and they are happy for me to borrow spades and pick axes whenever necessary, as long as I clean them off afterwards. There is nothing worse than leaving a spade full of clay in the farmyard for the next person to have to clean off before using it.

Early September saw me heading out onto the hills for the first time that season and the day dawned bright and sunny, though I could tell it was going to be a little too warm later on. I had a full compliment of terriers out that day and the dew on the ground would at least mean a holding scent for a while, until the sun rose higher into the sky. I parked at a local public house car park and walked up the steep road until it gave out onto a bridle track, which took me onto the top of Old Bruntwood Fell; a heather-clad hill that is a good spot for foxes. There is a crag earth down by the side of a ghyll, just above it, and there I found the feathers of a woodcock that had been freshly eaten, though the den was vacant.

There had been a serious decline in ground-nesting birds during more recent years and so I had decided to hunt this area quite extensively in order to get them returning to this place, for I was certain that a large population of the vulpine race was to blame for the lack in certain species of bird. I modelled my efforts on a pack of hounds and would disturb both earth and covert in order to prevent them from packing and in order to get them to go to ground, for they rarely will if undergrowth affords safer shelter, even during the winter months.

When I first came to this area and gained permission to try it, I was amazed to find foxes packing in separate locations. My terriers regularly flushed four, five and six foxes from brambles and bracken beds. However, I had kept up the pressure and had disturbed the places they chose to lie up and rarely did I find more than two foxes together any more, which just goes to show that my methods were working.

I dropped down into the valley and, at the foot of the fell, the small pack of earth dogs hit off a line and they cast all around, finally finding their scent and following out onto Middle Fell, where they hunted the line, almost together, through the deep heather. I hoped it had laid up here, but it hadn't and so they soon emerged out onto the hill grasses at the other side and then dropped down into the valley, following a sheep trod to the old drovers road and then over into the bracken-clad hillside above the beck. There was a two-holed earth here, but it was empty and they carried on, emerging back onto the old drovers road, where they had a check, and rather a bad one at that. I was soon on the spot, despite the fast pace, and cast in a wide circle. The move succeeded and they hit off again, going at a cracking pace across the scrub-pasture until they reached Chimney Gorse, above the road they had come to earlier. Scent was confusing here, as the fox must have hunted all over this area, especially among the rushes, so I cast back towards Bottom Reeds and away they went, leaving me to the rear as they rushed 'forrard' into the old ruins of Bruntwood Mill. Rock and Ghyll had led mostly, but Bella and Crag also played an important part in the proceedings and it was Bella who now led them out of the ruins and up to yet another old road, one that was used when the mill was in full production, and into the gorse bushes along here, where rabbits foiled the line.

I had stopped hunting rabbits for a season or two, as Myxi had hit them hard in recent years and numbers were so low that it was pointless controlling them. There were too few to be of any real nuisance to anyone, so I preferred to leave them well alone until numbers increased to a problematic population again. But still, a few were in among the bushes and the terriers were distracted and chased them out. After some time, I managed to cast them out the other side of the bushes and, sure enough, our fox had taken this route, for they were away, following a strong scent to a popular fishing spot that is surrounded by hills. They followed along the edge of the reservoir and then to the foot of a steep fell, climbing through the heather and into the bracken. They soon emerged and dropped back into the vale, but scent became difficult now after fifty minutes of exciting hunting and they struggled to follow. I cast them all around, but scent had faded quite a bit, due to the day at last warming up with the rising sun. However, the terriers speaking keenly heralded a fox on the run and, sure enough, I could see it running in front of the pack, having risen from its couch among the large tussocks of grass close to a wood and quickly putting some distance between itself and its pursuers.

They hunted it quite well around the wood and out the other side, onto the opposite hill, but, as they neared the old quarry and got out onto more exposed ground, then scent became difficult and it wasn't long before my terriers were returning to me. I knew it was pointless carrying on with this fox and so went on to draw elsewhere. I headed up a wild and remote valley and the terriers entered the large bracken bed on Hound Tor. It was obvious they were onto something and muffled cries meant they were to ground, so I went to investigate, for I knew of no earths here. Sure enough, close to the top of the bracken, they had entered a two-holed earth and by the sound of it a fox was at home. Rock was in pole position and her quarry had got itself into a tight spot under a small tree, which grew precariously on the steep hillside. Frustrated, the other terriers looked for another way to get ahead of Rock, but they found themselves grabbed by myself and quickly put on the couples and pegged down a little distance away, where they made quite a fuss. The farm lay just over the hill and I was there within minutes, borrowing a spade and pick, for I knew that this fox was going nowhere. A mark on the receiver box indicated three feet of earth to get through (I always put a collar on Rock before beginning a day's hunting, for she was often first to her quarry. Even if another beat her to it, I could still get a mark before she would emerge, looking for another way in), but the roots would undoubtedly make the going more than a little difficult.

The top surface of soil was easy going, but, unfortunately, compacted clay lay underneath and this was made even more difficult by the tangle of grass roots I had to cut through. A pick was necessary, rather than just a spade, and I was forced to break the clay up before removing it. This was painfully slow work, but it had to be done. I do not like using a pick-axe during digs, as a misjudgement could mean serious injury, possibly death, to a terrier working below, though a reading on a locator made the use of such tools far safer. Once I was a couple of feet down I simply hacked away at the clay to a much shallower depth and removed it more carefully. The sound of Rock baying grew louder with each spade-full of earth, clay and root I took out and the last few inches would see me going very gently indeed. In the meantime, the other terriers were mad keen to get and they made their desire plainly heard, despite my efforts to shut them up.

I poked away at the earth and broke through at last, directly behind my bitch, who carried on undaunted, maybe with even more zeal now that fresh air rushed into the tunnel. I had to carefully dig away the clay from above her body and head and was forced to use the pick at times, the going was that difficult, especially as I cleared around the roots of the tree, but always with a restraining hand, making certain that I gently hacked at the roof of the tunnel. This took quite some time and, by the time I had cleared enough room, she had finished a young fox from that year's fresh crop. It was fully-grown, but was lacking the trademark magnificent brush, owning a rather thin and straggly one, with its bones as yet not covered by full flesh and muscle. It was quite small and couldn't match the larger terrier, but still, Rock had a few bites and needed cleaning up at the beck in the valley bottom. This having been done, I back-filled as best I could on that steep hillside and then, as I stood up, I lost my balance and fell headlong down the hill, doing rather a good impression of a circus performer.

I fell around thirty feet in all, doing at least a couple of somersaults, but somehow managed to land on my feet. I was rather disorientated, but I still managed to look around me as though I had just fallen at a shopping precinct full of people, but only the terriers had seen my embarrassing escapade, though, just for a split-second, probably because my head hadn't yet cleared, I thought I could detect them having a little giggle at my expense!

I took my small pack home immediately and gave Rock a thorough clean. I put her in the bath and showered her with lightly warmed water, making certain that I washed her muzzle of all debris from that earth, while avoiding getting water into the eyes and ears, then gave her a thorough rub down with an old towel, before placing her in front of the fire. And then I washed the bites with boiled water that had cooled until just warm, which had been lightly salted (for bites near to the eyes I always use just cooled boiled water), wiping the muzzle with cotton wool. This I did four times a day for a few

I am sure the terriers had a giggle at my expense!

days and then I left the wounds to dry up. If they had been more serious, then penicillin injections, or a course of antibiotics, would have been necessary. The eyes often get bits of soil in them and a good eye wash from a local pet store will help clean them up. Wash them out first with cooled boiled water, using cotton wool to gently remove any debris, then put in the eye drops. This gives much relief to a terrier, which can be very miserable when muck is irritating the eyes. Diligent care is essential for working terriers!

During August, or early September, most packs of hounds start hunting again and this was formerly known as 'cub-hunting'. And then the term was changed to 'autumn-hunting', which is a time for teaching young hounds their true vocation in life. They learn to stick close to their Huntsman whilst hacking to the meet, or the first covert, and to enter the wood, gorse, crop, or any other suitable place where a fox may be found lurking, when asked and encouraged to do so. They also learn to come out of covert rather swiftly when the Huntsman requires it, usually after a fox has made a bid for open ground. And, of course, they learn to find, hunt and kill foxes, which is essential if farmers, keepers and landowners are to be kept happy.

The autumn is a time of learning for young hounds and the older, more experienced members renew their skills too and often improve in their own abilities, but it is also a time of learning for young foxes. They quickly learn that the sound of the horn signals danger and many will leave covert and be away, while others will be alert to danger and exit their home before hounds are upon them. Also, because foxes have such a strong survival instinct, they will be prevented from forming packs and hunting over the same ground, which would bring a lot of hardship on those who rear livestock for a living, when their coverts are disturbed and they are driven out. They then lead more nomadic lives, usually remaining within a territory, but one that ranges far and wide and a fox will often live alone, for much of the year anyway, except for the courting season from around December onwards when they can be found in pairs.

The professional terrierman begins his more traditional role during the late summer/early autumn period, as many young foxes will go to ground, rather than make for open country. This is often their undoing, for some are dug out and shot, if the landowner requires it, and the carcass given to young hounds, in order to reinforce their desire to hunt such quarry.

The less adventurous of foxes will often pay the price in full, for they will either go to ground and be dug out, or they will be caught by hounds. If they will not leave their refuge in covert, or they are not alert to danger, then they will often be accounted for. Some youngsters learn very quickly indeed and they get out of there rather swiftly. These are born survivors and will often go on to give hounds long runs when the season opens proper in November (October in the fell country). Others will hang around and be quickly 'chopped' by hounds. Some are sick and these fall prey within minutes, though that is a good thing, for it prevents a great deal of suffering and the spread of disease.

This time of the year sees many litters of cubs being dispersed and they will often leave their litter mates, even their mother, for good, once autumn-hunting begins in earnest. Young foxes are harried about the country, but they learn valuable survival skills. Also, because a pack of hounds prevents packs of foxes from forming, they do wildlife such as ground-nesting birds a rather valuable service, for less foxes hunting over an area means much more of a chance of escape, especially during the breeding season when eggs and young birds can fall prey to predators. The idea of packs is in order to improve the survival chances of each individual. Foxes use their noses to hunt, far more than any other sense, though sight and sound does play a part, constantly testing the wind for scent and following when such is discerned. A single fox can hunt effectively, but a pack will stand a far better chance of both detecting prey and accounting for it. So a pack of foxes could quickly and easily wipe out a population of ground-nesters, as well as hares, which live entirely in the open.

In one area where foxes were packing due to busy roads not allowing hounds access, as many as twelve were seen hunting through a valley and an acquaintance of mine lost his entire stock of chickens to them. Once I began hunting the coverts and running terriers through the earths the packing stopped and I have never found more than two together since, as in other areas. This allows other species of wildlife to thrive. Although much of the problems associated with low ground-nesting bird populations are to do with intensive farming, predation by foxes is also a problem. The songbird population is currently in serious decline and is not recovering in areas where habitat has been put aside, so this can only mean that predators are to blame. Magpies and grey squirrels will take eggs and young birds from nests, though foxes can also get among some of the bird species which nest lower down, such as thrushes and blackbirds. And, if hares are scarce, then one can be certain that a high fox population is killing leverets in the spring, as well as some adult hares.

Control is essential if other species are to prosper, though control should not be carried out to an extent that means foxes become scarce. Enough control to prevent packing and large numbers hunting over an area is the correct balance, though some do attempt to wipe out every individual in the district. Most of this country was keepered at one time, especially during the 19th century, and strict predator control measures meant that the songbird population prospered enormously. When keepered land became less and less, mainly after the First World War and again after the second, then such control was carried out to a much less degree. Couple this with intensive farming and pesticide use and is it any wonder that we are seeing many species of our valuable wildlife suffering depleted numbers to a very serious extent?

True, some keepers carried out pest control to such an extent that they would not tolerate predators on their land at all, while others were more sensible and enjoyed seeing predators around their beat, as long as they were not allowed to proliferate to such numbers that other species of wildlife suffered badly. This was a much more balanced approach and it worked. Wildlife prospered on these country estates and many also preserved foxes to some extent, for when the local hunt had a meet in the area. Several keepered estates were famous for their fox-holding coverts, though, of course, fox control was still carried out at such places, but without attempting to kill every single beast that hunted over the land, as was the attitude of some keepers.

There were also many famous earths on keepered estates and very often the gamekeepers would 'stop' these, saving the earth-stopper a job, when hounds were about to hunt over their land. Earth-stopping continued to be practised up until the hunting ban of 2005 and this was often carried out by a professional terrierman, though in some cases farmers and gamekeepers would stop the earths on their land, or at least open them up again after hunting had finished for that day. This served the purpose of keeping a fox above ground and was in no way useful in terms of control, except where an earth was a bad place where it was unwise, or even illegal (such as a badger sett) to enter a terrier. Foxes are clever and know of any safe refuge they can use, so stopping such places was essential if control was to be carried out.

I was a friend of an old earth-stopper who recently died and I found his tales of his times wandering the countryside and blocking fox earths fascinating. Many, especially during earlier centuries, would stop earths at night, but the majority of modern day earth-stoppers would carry out their duties during the afternoon prior to the day's hunting. Terriers would be used

A terrier makes certain an earth is empty.

A terrier evicting the tenant.

A terrier checks a drain for occupation.

in order to make certain that the earths were empty, or any tenants evicted, and these had to be trustworthy dogs that were totally reliable. Finding was an essential quality in an earth-stopper's terriers and this ability was vital, no matter how vast the den. And some earths are huge. Drains, for instance, are good places in which to find foxes and there are many up here in the Pennines. I know of several good drains that usually hold foxes and, while some are easily diggable, being up to around two-feet deep and with slabs of stone which easily lift off once the soil has been cleared away. Others are notoriously difficult, with pipes branching off in all directions and tunnels sometimes lying one on top of another.

Finding the location of an earth dog is a nightmare in such dens, even with locators, but in the old days when the 'ear to the ground' method was employed, it was nigh-on impossible. Drains, especially those made of pipes, distort sound and this can be very deceiving. On more than one occasion I have dug down, only to find that the terrier and quarry are far from the spot from where the sound seemed to be coming. In my own bit of country, on the edge of what is now the East Lancashire Railway, there is a notorious drain and my own terriers have been to ground in there with not a sound from them, despite the fact that they have been chasing foxes around the place for an age. There is a square with several pipes going off in all directions and one of them drops down the railway embankment and then runs along the edge of the railway for goodness knows how long a distance. Terriers seemed to work the place safely enough (when the railway was unused and abandoned to nature), but bolting foxes just didn't seem possible. There are that many tunnels that foxes can just keep on giving terriers the run around until they get fed up and finally emerge, which can sometimes take hours, so I gave up working this spot years ago.

The earth-stopper told me tales of his times wandering the countryside during the previous afternoon to the day's hunting and trying his terriers, Jack Russells in the main, at every likely spot. They could bolt several foxes during each afternoon, while at other times none could be found below ground. At other times badgers would be encountered and he would then have some hard and long digs in order to recover his earth dogs. These were not badger setts, however, but fox earths that had been used by 'Brock' probably just for that day. Maybe because it had wandered too far from home when the sun began to lighten the eastern sky, or maybe while it was wandering in search of establishing a territory for itself, where it would likely take over an old abandoned sett. Badger digging was legal then anyway, so he had no worries about engaging in such activities.

Another earth-stopper I knew would carry out his duties in much the same way, during daylight hours, rather than stumbling around in the darkness, though, if a fox would not bolt, he would dig it out and shoot it, if his Nuttall bred Patterdales hadn't already finished the job. He took quite a few foxes this way, but only because his country was well foxed and he knew there were plenty of others for the hunt. He didn't inform the hunt he worked for of his methods, of course, but they were appreciated by the local keepers and farmers.

Earth-stopping terriers are traditionally of the baying type and such are best suited to this type of work. A terrier that mauls and kills its quarry isn't really suited to such work, for foxes are required to be bolted unharmed when engaging in this activity and the stand off and bay variety is ideal for the task.

I have done a little earth-stopping during my earlier years of terrier work, though it wasn't for the local hunt. The lads I dug with would all converge on one area and we would have maybe four or five terriers and two or three lurchers with us, but we found that many of the foxes simply headed to the old mineshafts high on the steep hill and from there they just wouldn't shift, so we took to blocking the earths in order to keep foxes out. There were only four holes to block and this was quite easy, though I would run my terriers through, just to make certain that none were going to be blocked in. If run in by lurchers, they wouldn't bolt and one or two of the harder terriers we had with us would finish a fox below ground, but it was risky entering them into this place; for fear of a fall in of shale whilst the terrier engaged its foe, or maybe a rotten support would collapse, smothering the antagonists. But, if previously undisturbed, we sometimes succeeded in bolting one or two from here when stopping the holes.

I remember on one occasion, during a bitter cold winter afternoon with snow flurries on the wind and a dusting on the ground, when I entered Rock and Bella when they were both still young and very game. They went like wild fire and I knew then that a fox was home. It was freezing on that hillside and, because these shafts are vast in area, some going for anything up to a mile into the hills, so local folk say, it took some time for anything to happen and the cold crept inexorably right into my bones. But then, after quite some time, I heard pieces of shale falling inside the earth after being disturbed and suddenly a large fox bolted from the cold, dark entrance and it ran off across the rough ground ribbed with snow, finally disappearing into the

The old Earthstopper.

Nuttall bred Patterdales at his kennels.

deep heather. I had no lurcher with me, but one could not have negotiated this hillside with the same agility of a fox anyway and so pursuit would have been futile.

I watched Reynard as he emerged in the valley bottom and made his way south until he was gone from view; and then another shot out of the earth and was away, more or less in exactly the same direction. Rock emerged some time later, but Bella was gone until well into the night, no doubt chasing a third fox all over that huge earth, when she finally emerged and climbed up the hill to where I stood shining my torch, after hours to ground. I have no doubt that this third fox also bolted, but it was impossible to see and the wind muffled any noise that would have betrayed Reynard's presence. It was now too dark to stop the old shafts, but, after having been disturbed by the terriers they would hopefully keep out of that place for at least the next few days anyway.

Mineshafts are not the place in which to attempt to dig foxes, though on one rare occasion Pep, my Jack Russell bitch, did bottle one up in a stop end that was quite close to the main entrance, though it was deep and the going incredibly difficult. I never purposely enter a terrier into shafts anymore, and haven't done for many years, but in those early days I always ran terriers through this place, though my Jack Russell was a little weak in such enormous locations and she would only go so far before returning. On this occasion she entered the den and began baying only seconds later. We quickly located the spot and began digging, for it was soon obvious that this fox wasn't for bolting.

We cleared quite a large square and soon had piles of shale out of the ground, with an ever-deepening hole as we made our way towards the gallant bitch, rather more slowly, the further in we dug. Loose shale and soil is a nightmare to dig and is almost as bad as sand. I hate digging in sand and will not enter a terrier into such an earth, but it is not always possible to tell when an earth is sandy. The entrance holes may well look to be made up of nothing but soil, until one begins digging and maybe a foot into the earth one comes upon almost pure sand. Sand earths are notorious spots for suffocating working terriers, for the sides of tunnels are very much unstable and can collapse at any time. Shale and soil mixed is another type of earth that is very unstable and this became more and more obvious the deeper we went.

After hours of back breaking digging we finally broke through to the bitch and could just about see her at her fox. We had dug to the side of the crag that looms over the old shafts and she was under the overhang. But attempting to open up the hole in order to extract Pep and her quarry was proving impossible, as the shale kept rushing in again and again and filling what we had just taken out. There were still another two feet or so in depth before we could reach our quarry and, in the end, we had to give it up as a bad job, for the roof of the dig was looking more and more unstable, unpredictable, and it would have taken just one large rush in to have killed my terrier. The risk wasn't worth it and so, after over five hours of exhausting work, I managed to call out my bitch and then we back-filled, giving our fox best. When working terriers one must be philosophical, for, especially when one can dig few foxes from dug-out rabbit holes and rockpiles and crag earths make up much of the territory, quite a number will have to be left for another day.

I had merle with me that day and I can remember him trying to get into that tunnel in order to pull out the fox he knew to be lurking underneath. He once got to ground in a drain, when my terrier, Pep, was baying at her fox, and I had to dive into the entrance and grab his tail in order to prevent him getting any further.

This drain was one of the many that are made up of stone and some are quite large, but still, I was surprised that he could get his frame into such a tight space and actually crawl up the tunnel. He wasn't for coming out, either, but I held on grimly to his tail and shouted some rather stern warnings and eventually he began backing out, knowing he was beaten. If he had gone right in, then I am certain we would have been digging a large part of that drain out in order to free him. Merle originally belonged to a neighbour and was called Radar, would you believe! As he grew I could see he was a lurcher, though rather a heavily built one, and he was always out on the street playing with the local children. I had a greyhound, Bess, at the time, as well as Pep, the Jack Russell, which made up quite a mixed bobbery pack when I got together with two or three fellow hunters, but still, I wanted another dog. I pestered my mum and she finally relented. I asked if I could have the dog, which was hardly ever in the house anyway, and the neighbour agreed. That is how I came to own one of the best dogs I have ever seen at work. He only ever caught one hare during his career, but he could hunt like a hound, would mark fox earths with unflinching accuracy, would take and kill those that bolted, was a superb lamping and ferreting dog and ratted as keenly as any terrier. Though it took some time for him to settle in, now that he wasn't allowed to wander the streets. I changed his name immediately and took my inspiration from Brian Plummer's famous lurcher.

He was very well socialised, as a result of wandering the streets and encountering cats, other dogs and, of course, people, children in particular, but he did have some bad habits. The first thing I did was to stop him wandering the streets immediately and this made him more than a little frustrated at times. He would sometimes sneak upstairs if the living room door wasn't shut properly and I would find a book pulled off the shelves and it would be partly chewed. There was little I could do about it, as I hadn't seen who was the culprit, though I had strong suspicions as to who was to blame.

I came home one day and found Merle gone, with the living room door slightly ajar, so I crept upstairs and, sure enough, there was my lurcher just pulling one of my best books off the shelves in order to have a good old chew. I burst into the room and startled the dog, picking up the book and hitting him with it, though, of course, the blow wasn't too hard. He slunk away downstairs with a barrage of abuse in his ear and I made it plain enough that he was in the 'doghouse' for a while. This may not be a method endorsed by the 'experts' and 'animal behaviourists', but it was one that worked with immediate effect, for he never chewed a book again, nor anything else for that matter, and his training continued with few problems. I still have that book and the teeth marks are still there, reminding me of my faithful, hardworking lurcher, Merle.

He entered to rabbit and rat very quickly and was keen on fox soon after. But, by the 1990s he was an old dog and he had slowed down quite considerably, though he was still keen and would have a go. I remember one day when I was out walking and Rock went to ground at a large rockpile that rarely held a fox at that time, though in more recent years it has become quite a popular spot and a fox can regularly be found there. It was quite a windy day and I could hear nothing until, suddenly, a fox bolted right at my feet and was away over the rocks, with my ageing lurcher quickly in pursuit. He did well for an old dog, but, as the run went on, the fox managed to keep ahead of him and eventually it pulled away and escaped. It was sad seeing one of my most reliable workers in decline and I knew that he must be retired, though he certainly wasn't happy about that, for he continued to hunt and often put rabbits up, or hunted a fox, while out at exercise.

One day he put a rabbit out of a hedge and was quickly in action, chasing it across the field towards the ancient wood where drains and burrows were used by coney. But, like that fox, the rabbit pulled ahead of him and he

Digging is difficult at some places.

Many earths are made up of rockpiles.

yelped in frustration as the run continued. The rabbit made the safety of the wood, but still Merle carried on, putting his nose to the ground and hunting the line in typical fashion. It was a sad sight, when formerly he would have buried that rabbit before it had got half way across the field.

He was quite a character and got up to quite a bit of mischief and I can remember one day when I was watching a kestrel's nest as the parents returned time and again with food for the growing youngsters. The nest was high on a wall of an old factory and the activity there could easily be seen, so I moved in for a closer look. I had Merle with me that day and, as I walked, I kept my eye on the nest and the parent bird busily feeding a fast growing chick. The trouble was, I wasn't watching where I was going and that had been one of the 'rules of life' that had been drummed into me as a kid. Whenever I fell, or bumped into something, my attempts to gain sympathy would all be in vain and all I got for my troubles, despite some rather painful injuries at times, was, ' yuh should watch where yer goin'.' I had failed to heed this oft' repeated advice yet again and failed to see a deep ditch in my way. I focused fully on the scene enacted above and suddenly fell headlong into the ditch, the ground simply disappearing from under my feet. As if that wasn't enough of an indignity, Merle then proceeded to jump on top of me, thinking a game was afoot, and clamped his powerful jaws over my flat cap, pulling it violently from my head and taking a nice chunk of hair with it. He then ran off with his prize and wouldn't give it back, no matter how I cajoled him, for quite some time. I would approach as he dropped the cap, barking defiance at his master, but then, when I was rushing in and bending down to pick it up, he would then rush in, grab it and run off with it once more, enjoying such a wonderful game of 'torment'. He did eventually drop the cap and leave it alone, but kept well out of my way for some time afterwards. The kestrels had been going about their normal daily business, when all of a sudden I had loomed up, fallen into a ditch, been pounced on by a mad dog and had then come out of there, covering a newly acquired bald patch with my hand on my head and screaming death threats at the lurcher. It had all been too much for them and the parents had flown away by this time. And so I got out of there rather sharpish, not wishing to risk them abandoning their fledglings, which may have happened had I hung around for too long.

Gary and I were out again and Tiny was alongside the terriers. They entered a large bracken bed that held quite a bit of low growing shrubbery and, sure enough, a fox was in residence. I cover quite a bit of high country,

mainly made up of moorland and fell, but today we were hunting the woodland and pastures of the low country and it made a welcome change. There are plenty of foxes in these areas and they are a little fatter and a little slower than the moorland variety, though they are still difficult to catch. The terriers flushed their quarry and Tiny was quickly in action, bearing down on his fox and snatching it from the ground as it made a bid to escape. Tiny was a big powerful lurcher and a quick shake broke Reynard's neck and it died very quickly indeed, without really suffering, or, indeed, knowing much about what had occurred. The terriers had a taste of the carcass and then were away again.

The bracken, trees and shrubs were tinted with the coming colours of autumn and the wind held a chill that betrayed the inevitable coming of winter, but the sun shone through the slowly drifting clouds on regular occasions and we were reminded that summer had only recently ended. Late September is a most enjoyable time to be out. It is not usually warm enough to be uncomfortable, nor is it too cold either. It is just right and a dry day at this time of year is just perfect for being out and about after Reynard. The little pack of earth dogs hunted up the valley and they cast at every likely spot, putting rabbits up in places, though still not in very large numbers, despite the past summer breeding season. There were none with myxi, for the moment anyway, which was quite a relief, but still, I would not ferret them when they were not in large enough numbers to be considered a pest.

The terriers were spread out over that hillside, with Rock high up among the trees and it was she who flushed the fox and hit off its line, her loud bay sounding among the undergrowth, which sent the rest of the pack scurrying to her rather rapidly. They took up the line and hunted keenly along the hillside, sometimes in view, at other times obscured by the trees, bracken, brambles, nettles, or anything else that would afford the fleeing quarry a bit of cover. They went towards the cinder earths above and I was just a little worried, lest Reynard had gone to ground here, but they quickly passed them by and carried on up the valley. I have never known a fox to be in these earths, though local tales tell of a terrier that was lost here many years ago, maybe after the roof of the dig fell in, for cinders quickly loosen and collapse in such earths, which, thankfully, are rarely encountered.

Gary and I saw our fox soon afterwards, as it made its way down the valley and away into the wood. The pack followed the scent with hardly a check and we then lost them, having to search for their whereabouts. A whimper below a long line of trees on top of the hill captured our attention and we headed there immediately. Sure enough, Reynard had gone to ground here, at what looked like a dug-out rabbit hole, and the rest of the pack were frustrated because of not being able to get up to their quarry. Ghyll had the lead place and he was hard at his fox, though this dig wasn't going to be easy. Gary went back to the car and fetched digging tackle, while I pegged down the terriers, once they had emerged.

The dig, indeed, was very hard going and then the inevitable compacted clay was soon encountered, as were the tree roots, which added to our difficulties. The ground was dry too, this being late September, before the autumn rains had begun to fall, and also because the tree roots quickly sapped any moisture in the ground. Dry ground is difficult to dig through and we were soon down to our T-shirts, despite the chilled breeze.

Ghyll was a jealous sort, this being accentuated because he was young and still relatively inexperienced, and he soon fell silent, which, I was sure, meant that he had killed his quarry, but would not leave it, reluctant to give it up to the others. We carried on digging, however, and at one point Ghyll was going to emerge, but the sight of us and the sound of the nearby dogs made him possessive again and he went back to his dead quarry. It took us seven hours of toil to reach him that day, due entirely to clay and tree roots and dry ground, but we eventually uncovered a dog fox and the jealous terrier unwilling to give up his prize. It had been a hard dig, but well worthwhile and, after back-filling, I took Ghyll home and cleaned up his wounds, which were not too serious at all and they soon healed without any problems. In fact, I think I suffered most, for an old injury to my right elbow was giving me some stick after that long and tedious dig.

We had spent the late summer and early part of autumn flushing and dispersing foxes from several different coverts, leaving many of them unharmed, but taking out a few, in order to ensure that effective control was carried out. I do not believe in killing large numbers of foxes, as roads, other dogs and guns will account for quite a large number, though I still like to do my bit for local farmers. And so catching some with the lurcher, or digging some, was essential, if the local landowners were to be kept happy, otherwise they would not have us on their land. Sometimes we even managed to catch a fox or two above ground with the terriers and these were either foxes dumped from towns, or they were sick, maybe even injured.

I was again hunting the low country made up of woodland and pasture and, at the edge of Mill Wood, Ghyll went into covert in such a manner as to betray the presence of quarry lurking somewhere within. Sure enough, he quickly found and a battle royal took place. And then a fox bolted out of the covert. It was a poor specimen indeed, straggly, with lifeless fur and a thin brush and Ghyll ran it down inside the wood in next to no time. I was soon on the spot and knocked the poor creature on the head, killing it instantly. There were no signs of mange, but it was obviously in a bad state of health and was, I believe, one that had been dumped by 'do-gooders' after being caught in a nearby town, or maybe in the city of Manchester. Just exactly what these people think they are achieving I do not know, but they are bringing problems on these foxes as most either get taken with dogs, are snared, or they are shot. They are not 'street-wise' in a country sense, for they do not have the same fear of dogs as country foxes and that is why they are easily caught. They have no reason to be trap, or snare, shy, nor do they have much fear of people, thus they can quickly be accounted for using a gun. The farmer has troubles from such foxes too, as they have no idea about catching wild game and will instead go for the easier option; that of farm reared livestock, lambs in the spring, or chickens and ducks at any time of the year. Town foxes can often 'boss' dogs and they have been known to attack them. I have seen them stand their ground out in the country, showing no fear of the approaching dog, but then they have received a severe shock as the terrier/lurcher/hound goes in for the kill without any preliminary warning. Some are so ill that they cannot run and it is a kindness to knock them on the head and put them out of their misery instantly.

Young foxes are often encountered during the autumn months and they are easily distinguishable from more mature foxes. One was found to ground in a drain which is only a five minute walk from my house and it was rather convenient, for a Jack Russell bitch, Snatch, had recently come to my kennels and I was entering her to fox for a friend. She was a tidy bitch and had done well in puppy classes at shows that summer, but now it was time for her to be entered to quarry and I took her out that day with my old and faithful bitch, Rock.

I headed down into the valley with little hopes of finding a fox in this drain, as it had never held for the past few years, despite it being an ideal type of earth. It was a stone drain and many of these are easy enough, being two feet deep and having convenient slabs of stone covering them, which can so easily be lifted off once the soil was cleared, though this particular drain was an unknown quantity. I had dug several of them before and so I knew them intimately, but, as I said, I had never found Reynard at home here before now.

Rock among the autumn cover.

A small pack of terriers from Stan Mattinson's strain.

A fox bolted from an earth by the side of the Queen's Head, Troutbeck,
by a Coniston terrier belonging to Anthony Chapman.
Hounds lost it soon after.

Rock entered an earth, or a covert, in such a manner that told you Reynard was in residence, in spite of the fact that she had hardly had time to test the entrance for scent. I knew immediately that she had found and she scrambled up the dark passage and began baying and tackling her fox. I soon had a mark on the locator, up a steady incline about twenty feet from the entrance. Surprisingly, the reading was around five feet in depth, which was a little unusual, but not unknown. Some drains I have dug have been several feet in depth and many are not the 'easy dig' one first imagines. However, my bitch was hard at her quarry and this was a perfect opportunity for the young Russell. I allowed her to go in and out as she pleased for a while and she would join in for a few minutes and then emerge, wondering what it was all about, but that didn't worry me, for both Rock and Ghyll had acted in a similar way during their first digs and they had blossomed into superb terriers.

I had to cut through the tangle of grasses first and I dug out a neat square that would give me enough room as I got deeper. It is worth spending time digging out quite an area to begin with, for one can easily get carried away and rush a job. I have been guilty of this myself on several occasions, wanting to dig down as quickly as possible, but then getting to such a depth that one is stifled for room. In this situation the only thing to do is to go back to the start of the dig and take out a lot more soil in order to open up the trench and create more space. This took quite some time and darkness was already beginning to creep across the land as the sun sank behind the hills away to the west. I had started late afternoon and the dig was not at all easy. I was on my own and needed to rest at times, so progress was slow and I feared I would be beaten by the onset of darkness. Rock was still hard at her quarry and I attempted to speed progress a little, but the going was difficult as I cut through years of compacted earth and removed sometimes-large boulders out of that slowly deepening trench.

The sun crept inexorably behind the Pennine hills to the west and it became more and more difficult to see what I was doing. I could hear Rock not far below and she had a hold on her quarry now, possibly throttling it. And, sure enough, soon afterwards she emerged, having finished the job before I could break through. She had a few bites on her muzzle, but it must have been one of that year's crop of young foxes and it had paid the price for not bolting and getting out of there. I didn't have time to carry on, for it would soon be as black as pitch, but I had about enough time to allow Snatch a taste of the quarry. She entered keenly, but no longer barked, tasting the carcass instead and remaining with it for a surprising amount of time. I back-filled rather quickly and, in the end, had to shout the bitch out of the earth. It had been a good experience for her, though I regretted coming out so late in the day and not being able to actually break through. But I was at least a foot off the roof of the drain and then I would have had to clear the soil from the slab which may have been up to two feet in length, so I had no chance of succeeding that day. I could have left the hole open till the morning and dug it out then, but I didn't see the point in that. I knew for sure that that fox had perished and the youngster had enjoyed herself and had gained a little valuable experience. Also, farm livestock may have wandered down there and fallen into the trench, so it is always the best policy to backfill during the same day whenever possible.

Snatch had seen her first fox to ground and had done okay for a first-timer. I have known terriers show no interest at all during even the first couple of digs, before something clicked and they began going at last. She had begun working cover by this time and had joined in when the others had flushed foxes from their chosen couch in the undergrowth, but there was nothing like traditional earth work to get a terrier going properly.

Her next taste of fox was above ground, after Ghyll had hunted what turned out to be another town fox that had been so thoughtlessly dumped in the countryside. We were hunting a wooded valley and I had out that day just Ghyll and Snatch, for it is good for a youngster to watch an experienced terrier at work and learn from it. I had checked the stone drain in the valley, but it was vacant and Ghyll turned away without showing the slightest bit of interest. He then headed up the hill and climbed out above the crags looming overhead, with the narrow strip of woodland clinging precariously to the tops of the rocky outcrops.

He then disappeared among the heather and the bronzed bracken and sometime later he spoke very keenly indeed. There were no rabbits in this area, especially up on those high tops, so I knew that a fox was afoot. And, soon after, this was confirmed when Reynard came bounding through the heather and ran right passed me, once he had scrambled down the crag, now running off down the valley in a southerly direction. Ghyll was soon on the spot and hunted his fox eagerly, with Snatch joining in the fun and disappearing down the valley in hot pursuit. They eventually lost their quarry, but, again, it had been a good experience for the Russell bitch and she was relaxing and enjoying herself more and more as she began to discern what life was all about.

Some digs can be slow and hard-going.
This was the end of a two-day dig.

Rock & Ghyll; both began a little slowly, but blossomed into fine workers.

Rock, after flushing 6 foxes from the bracken.

s.f.

s.f.

We carried on and, at the edge of the wood, Ghyll began showing interest at some low-growing brambles that were still laden with fruit, though it was now past its best. He entered the covert and was quickly onto a fox, though one that wasn't afraid enough to make a run for it, standing its ground instead and attempting to see off the terrier. It should have made a run for it. Ghyll had it by the throat in no time at all and was shaking it like a rat by the time I reached him, after fighting my way through that tangle of prickly branches. It was near dead and a hard blow to the head finished it instantly, then I picked it up in order to have a closer look. It was as light as a feather and I could tell immediately that this was yet another town fox. It mustn't have been eating much at all of late and, indeed, hadn't grown much from when it was a cub. It was easy pickings for the big, powerful terrier, but many town foxes do not have the same fear of dogs and pay the price in full when dumped in the countryside. Snatch was allowed a taste of the carcass and then I left it in the middle of the undergrowth, out of sight of any passing ramblers. If terriers, lurchers or hounds do not account for such sad specimens, then they occasionally fall prey to farm collies, when they go in search of food at the nearest farmyard. Town foxes are naturally drawn to man's dwellings when dumped, simply because they associate such places with food, having scavenged leftover scraps in order to survive. But this usually lands them in trouble when out in the country.

Hounds occasionally 'chop' a fox in covert, that is, catch it before it has a chance of escape. I believe that many 'chopped' foxes are, in fact, either sick or injured specimens, or they are town foxes that have been dumped so thoughtlessly by 'do-gooders'. True, sometimes a healthy country fox can be caught 'napping', being unable to get away from hounds after they have managed to get so close to it. But that is very rare indeed, for foxes are alert creatures that have learnt to sleep 'with one eye open' at all times, in order to survive the many threats they face.

That fox was such a poor specimen that it hadn't even managed to bite Ghyll in retaliation. Few terriers can avoid being bitten when at work, especially if the fox is an adult and it is healthy and full of vitality, so it is important to practise good first aid when injuries are received. Fox bites can fester and it is surprising how quickly they become infected and begin smelling of putrid flesh.

The autumn is a very busy time for a pack of hounds and the appointed terrierman especially. Dispersal is accomplished at this time and the youngsters quickly learn to get out of there when they hear hounds nearby.

The sick, unadventurous, or lazy, foxes are accounted for, very often when they get to ground and are dug out, at the request of the landowner, and are then shot, rather than thrown to hounds as some may believe. True, this was practised by some packs many years ago, but they soon saw the error of their ways and began using much more humane methods. In fact, the hunting community, of its own accord, looked for ways of improving the welfare of the beasts they hunted without any legislation from government.

My own little pack of terriers had done a good job of dispersing this year's new crop of foxes and all of the coverts and earths had been disturbed, with fewer being found as the autumn progressed. Some had been using the earths and I had enjoyed a few good digs, with varying success, so far. If the coverts were not disturbed, then the foxes rarely went to ground and traditional terrier work was then almost non-existent. And so I busied myself with keeping foxes on the move, hunting and dispersing those I found above ground, while I dug out and killed those I found below, though some I bolted and then allowed the terriers to chase and hunt their quarry for as long as possible.

I have found that terriers do not need to taste carcasses continually in order to remain keen and reliable at work, though, of course, sometimes it is good for them to do so. It all depends on the area you hunt. If foxes are a real problem and the farmers use terriermen to control numbers, then killing quite a number is essential, but many of the farms where I have worked over the years have also allowed guns on and these can sometimes kill large numbers. And so I tend to allow a few foxes to escape under such circumstances, while still giving my terriers the work they need in order to remain keen and trustworthy and in order to progress with experience.

A hard terrier will kill a fox, or badly injure it, so I often dig with a baying type, such as Crag, or even Rock, for older foxes could stand their ground and come out of the encounter unharmed. I only ever recall her killing one adult fox and that was during a two-day stint to ground in a dug out rabbit hole. She had dug on up to her fox and the soil behind had blocked her exit, so she had to be rescued. Whether the fox had suffocated, or she had finished it, I do not know, but killing adult foxes was not her forte' at all, though finding and staying with those that didn't bolt certainly was. Bella was another hard terrier, though she wasn't used nearly as much as the others. She had been savaged by a dog as a pup and since then had attacked them, that is, any strange dog, before they could attack her, so it was more than a little awkward using her. She was fine in her own little pack, but any lurcher

An old fashioned fox terrier similar in stamp to Snatch.

she didn't know would be attacked if I wasn't quick enough to grab her. This fault made me wary of breeding from her too, so I never carried on the line, though it was one that couldn't be faulted for working ability.

November arrived and so did the frosts, the dead leaves lying crisp and covered in white crystals during several mornings. There were still plenty of leaves on the trees and the rich autumn colours could be seen everywhere, before the winds whipped up and stripped bare the hedgerows, spinneys, woodlands and forests. And then came the first of that year's snow. The sky was heavy with cloud when I went out to clean the kennels and give the terriers a run around the garden and soon afterwards a few flakes began to fall, being driven about on the icy breeze. A few flurries followed and then, as I pulled up outside Gary's house, the snow began falling in a steady stream, with some of the flakes being quite a size.

By the time we got to the foot of the hills and began driving up the narrow country lane that leads to the scattered farms, there was about half an inch covering on the ground and I was beginning to get a little worried about getting the car stuck. A few wheel spins occurred as we climbed ever higher, but it wasn't long before we pulled up and set off in search of foxes. The cold had really set in now and there was nothing like a fall of snow for getting Reynard to go to ground, so I was quite hopeful of a find.

Ghyll, Crag and Rock were out that day and Gary had brought along his terriers, Red, a fell type bitch, Jock, a Middleton bred Lakeland, and his lurcher, Tiny, though these were not very good conditions for a running dog. We tried all manner of earths and I was rather disappointed at not being able to find, but things began looking up when we arrived at an old quarry, where the terriers were keen at a rockpile. I loosed Ghyll and Rock and they entered the pile at different places. We were hoping for a dig here, as a bolt would probably escape in such rough surroundings, or at the very least, if we couldn't reach them, the two terriers would finish the job below. Sure enough, they found a fox, but this was a very difficult earth that was incredibly tight and it was soon obvious that the pair couldn't quite get up to their quarry. So it was coats off and Gary and I began digging into the stone-pile in order to try to open up the passage so that the earth dogs could get on. In soil they could have dug on themselves, but in unyielding rock they are going nowhere, so one must try to help where possible. I have known my terriers to dig at rock with such eagerness and frustration so as to make their paws bleed. When this occurs it is important to soak them in salted water two or three times a day until they heal. Sometimes pads split on rock too and the same treatment is very effective in such cases.

Rock was coming in at one side and Ghyll at the other and our quarry was somewhere inbetween, but they would come out and swap sides, looking for a better way to get, in their frustration. They were being driven wild with excitement and all the terriers were tried in turn, hoping that one would just be narrow enough to get through. Lakeland terriers were bred to be very narrow in the shoulders for just such reasons.

The old Bedlington type of fell terrier had two major faults. One, their coat was poor and many suffered badly during bad weather and, two, they were often quite large in the chest and couldn't quite get in some spots. Fox terrier blood was used in order to correct both of these faults and some of the early Lakelands were incredibly narrow and these were used in earths, usually borrans, where more 'chesty' types just couldn't get on. It is a well known fact that most of the fell packs kept early pedigree Lakelands for just such occasions, as well as for killing lamb worrying foxes, or those that went to ground late in the day and had to be accounted for. We could have done with one right now and a few years ago a friend of mine did own and work a pedigree Lakeland. Our own terriers, not quite so refined in the chest, couldn't squeeze through and a good couple of hours of digging, with the countryside becoming covered in a deeper white blanket as the day went on, had seen our efforts frustrated. We had hit large boulders that we were not going to shift and in the end we gave our quarry best.

There was just one last spot to try and this was at an old ruin that had once been a busy mill that had seen full production once the industrial revolution had taken hold. But now the walls had crumbled and little of its past glory remained, though some drains and stone-piles made useful places to try and we headed there, hopeful of another find. I tried a brick-lined drain next to the brook that I had found, or, rather, that my terriers had found when hunting mink during the summer, but it was empty and the terriers turned away without showing any interest. I had deemed that drain a sure find back in the summer, especially during a spell of cold weather, but it just shows how one can be so wrong and how unpredictable foxes can be. I have often marked certain earths as sure finds, only to have never found one in, during nearly thirty years of trying such places. And there are the other types of earth that one would consider unusable, such as those found alongside a busy footpath used regularly by dog walkers and ramblers. My terriers mark these regularly, but working such places isn't really practical, with the general public passing by at regular intervals. There is even a gap

An old Bedlington blooded fell terrier
with Arthur Irving's Lakeland.

An old Bedlington type fell terrier
belonging to Tommy Dobson.

in the stones on an old bridge that is the least likely spot to hold, yet I have found foxes in there on two occasions, though it usually holds rabbits.

I climbed the hill strewn with stones that had once been part of the mill in its former glory and, by the cobbled track that was once used to cart supplies to and from here, Ghyll marked a steel pipe and then ran round to where a gap led under a huge slab of York stone. He quickly disappeared below ground and bayed like fury. It all happened so fast that we were caught a little unawares and shortly after a large fox bolted from the pipe at speed, going down the steep bank and using the rough tumble of stone-piles in order to throw off the lurcher, which, frankly, didn't stand a chance over such bad country. What a sight though. A fox in full winter coat running across the uneven ground covered in a generous layer of snow, with some large flakes slowly descending still, the icy breeze nipping at our ears. We may have failed to catch both foxes, but that didn't matter too much. There would be other days, but a sight like that on such a day as this was not a common occurrence and I still have warm memories regarding that time. The terriers had worked very well and had played their part and the lurcher had enjoyed a good, if fruitless, run. Also, we had taken part in quite a long and difficult dig, so it was satisfying in more ways than one.

That fox had vacated the premises rather swiftly and Ghyll had no bites that needed treating. That first fox had kept well out of the way, knowing it was safe enough if it stayed put, so all of the earth dogs were unmarked and in fine fettle, which wasn't always the case after a day in the hills. Rock earths, especially when a fox gets in a very tight space, can be bad places for a terrier to work and some of mine have emerged, not only with quite a number of bites around their muzzle, but also with the fur taken off in places, particularly around the top of the head, their skin scratched from the jagged edges of the rocks. Stickpiles can also be tight places and I have seen my terriers emerge from such dens with large areas of fur stripped almost completely out, they have pushed on that far into a tight spot in order to reach their quarry. When scratched in rock, slightly salted water is again the preferred treatment, though, of course, not near the eyes, being applied three or four times a day for the best part of a week. Then allow the wounds to dry up, with maybe a clean once a day if you deem it necessary. I always use cooled boiled water, for this is much cleaner and will aid the healing process. When treating tender bites it is a good idea to gently dab at the wounds, rather than rub them. If there is a hole, rather than a gash, then use a syringe without the needle attached, in order to wash out the bite with salted water.

The snow lasted for exactly one day and was almost completely gone by the morning, except for where it still lay on the higher tops, particularly on the summits of the Southern Pennines away to the east. I was sad to see the snow melting away so soon after it had fallen, but never mind, for now we could get at the rats around farmyards, with the undergrowth having withered a great deal and especially after being flattened by the heavy snow. Runs and holes were more easily seen and it was time to tackle the rodent problem. One of the local farmers was clearing his cattle sheds of straw and left over feed and there were reputedly many rats burrowing into this haven of warmth and comfort. The pack of terriers had assembled on the outer edges of the outbuilding and the digger went into operation immediately. As soon as the machine moved forward and began digging into the large piles of straw, feed and muck, rats began erupting from every gap and the action began, fast and furious. A rat would be out and one of the terriers had it. Some got past the terriers and were either hit with sticks, or Tiny went into action and chased them down before they had got very far.

Terriers will often kill rats by shaking them violently while biting hard. This prevents a dog from being bitten, but it also completely disorientates the quarry and may, in some cases, result in a broken neck. This sort of killing often takes place when the odd rat bolts here and there. When they are spilling out all over the place, as in this case, then a powerful crushing bite is administered and the beast is then dropped, in order that another can be caught and dealt with. And on the action goes. The terriers would pick up a rat, bite and drop and then go after the next, sometimes for several moments at a time. The machine operator would stop and watch the fast and furious action and he seemed to be enjoying himself. If we needed a breather, or a rat had escaped that area and needed to be accounted for, then he would hold up for a few minutes, though rats would emerge in large numbers with each pile he tackled and moved.

A large rat ran past Snatch and she was in pursuit, having entered to this quarry from the start, though it got itself under a water trough along the outer wall of the building and we had to go poking around there trying to shift it. I had Titch and Jet with me, my two jill ferrets, and they were soon in action. At last they bolted our quarry, with about four terriers standing around, but it shot out of there that quickly that we were all taken by surprise, including the dogs, and it managed to get passed once again. Rats can move at speed, but the terriers were gaining on it, though a little too late, for it squeezed under the base of the wall and was gone, with the terriers, agile as they

Narrow shoulders and chest are needed when working rock.

Gary Middleton with
one of his Lakeland terriers.

Alan Johnston, of Oregill fame,
with a terrier bred partly from
pedigree Lakeland blood.

Barry Todhunter with his fell terriers.

were, unable to follow. They sniffed and snorted and looked for another way through in their frustration, but we moved them on, back to the digging site where the action began again.

A few rats did escape the immediate area of the best of the action, but later, with the heaps now devoid of skulking 'Rolands', we searched around the yards and the dogs marked at various places. They were keen under some old planks and wooden sheets and in went Titch, as keen as mustard, but 'Ratty' wasn't for moving and the ferret emerged shortly afterwards, with a couple of bites around her nose. Rats are well-armed creatures that can put up quite a defence when necessary and we guessed that this was a doe rat with either young, or a nest prepared for their imminent arrival. We shifted as much of the wood as was possible and, sure enough, came upon a nest made up mainly of hay and straw, but still devoid of a young family. The doe rat was quickly out at the other end and Crag had it soon after.

The pack marked a small outhouse and here were kept logs and bits and pieces of farm machinery. We managed to shift some of the rats, but others could not be got at and these had to be left. The ferrets bolted a few from the logs, but again a bite or two was received by these game little creatures which just carried on their work as though nothing had happened. A wash with cooled boiled water and a dab of iodine soon sorted them out and the ferrets then remained in their little container for the rest of the afternoon, while we attempted to bolt as many more as possible. Again the pack of earth dogs began marking, this time underneath a feeding trough and we were soon on the spot, doing our utmost to bolt the reluctant creature lurking underneath. It wasn't for coming out of there, however, but Crag had it, when its backside appeared for a brief moment. He shot underneath and dragged the 'varmint' out of there, before it met a very quick end.

They soon ran out of places to mark and it was then that we had a count up, after spending quite some time around the farm. There were over a hundred corpses piled up at the finish and the farmer was extremely pleased with such a good and fruitful result. Rats can cost farmers hundreds, sometimes thousands, of pounds in lost feed for their livestock and they can also chew at the structure of outbuildings and completely ruin them, so we knew we had done him a good service that day. With a population such as this, we deemed it worth checking out the local waterways close the farm, just in case they had spread out from there.

A few days later we were walking along the side of a nearby brook and the terriers were quickly in action again, with Rock and Bella marking a hole

Fell, after finishing his quarry in rock.
Note the fur taken completely off by the jagged edges.

Two old fashioned working Scottish terriers;
experts at working in rock.

on the bank. They dug like fiends and eventually got close to the rat, but, as I pulled them away in the hopes of bolting their quarry, it shot out and was through their legs before any of us had time to think, splashing into the water and disappearing downstream where it made good its escape. Rats are incredibly quick and agile creatures and can sometimes pull off spectacular escapes.

Rats were few and far between, most of them having remained at the farm, but we did account for a small number, after Jet bolted them from any warrens the dogs marked. At one spot she entered a lair and emerged soon after with several bites on her face, having killed a doe rat and her youngsters, so it was time to call it a day and treat those bites to avoid any infection. Jet was rarely bitten and was a very good ratter, but she would need a couple of weeks rest after this episode.

Rat bites heal very quickly indeed when cleaned thoroughly and diligently and the swelling can be down within twenty-four hours, so terriers can easily cope with a busy ratting schedule and we were out again soon after, at a hill farm belonging to the Robinson family. I had Titch with me that day, having decided to give Jet more time to heal, as well as a few terriers milling about eagerly, ready for any action they may be able to enjoy. They marked a stone wall on the outside of a building housing a huge bullock and I just hoped my ferret wouldn't emerge the other side, for I was non too keen on going in there in order to retrieve her!

Titch crept into the narrow passage and it was soon obvious that a rat was on the run. These dry-stone buildings, like dry-stone walls bordering fields, can be hollow in places and a rat, or, indeed, a rabbit in some areas, can give a ferret the run around for quite some time, before finally bolting, especially when they know dogs are awaiting their presence outside. So it was quite a while before the rat finally bolted and Ghyll had it, snapping it up before it had gotten far and killing it very quickly indeed. Titch soon appeared at the edge of the rough stones and was placed back in her little carrier. It wasn't long before they marked a well used warren at the back of the farm, close to the duck pond, and in went Titch, her tail bushed out and swishing from side to side as she went; a sure indication that 'ratty' is home.

This was a large warren and runs to and from indicated regular use, but it was quite some time before the action started. A large rat suddenly bolted, but, seeing the terrier at the end of its run, it turned swiftly around and shot back into the tunnel. However, it now faced a dilemma and decided it would rather make a bid at escape, than face the angry ferret, which was obviously

s.f.

We could now get at the rats.

on its way up the passage in hot pursuit, for the rat bolted again and almost got past Snatch, who had it just before it got under the fence. She shook violently and crushed it with her powerful jaws, being reluctant to give up her catch and keeping it in her mouth until Gary was able to prise it from her.

Two more bolted almost at the same time and a couple of terriers were in action, with one chasing and catching its quarry on the field, and the other getting away by running under a nearby chicken house. We marked the spot and would deal with that later, in the meantime rats were bolting much more frequently by now and at least a dozen came out of that warren, with a couple escaping. All were large adults and all the terriers had a share in accounting for them. Rock was still at the pen where the rat had escaped earlier, marking keenly, and Titch soon had it from under that structure. It ran right into Bella and she finished it extremely quickly, before it could reach one of the main outbuildings of the farm. We were asked to try the barn and ferreted some likely places, but the walls and under the floor was that hollow that it was impossible to bolt them and the ferret could only chase in vain, until she eventually emerged after getting more than a little fed up with the whole thing. A scout around the yard and buildings yielded a few more rats, but this place certainly wasn't overrun with them. We had quite severely dented the population by now, I was sure, so left feeling satisfied that we had done a good job and a worthwhile service to the farmer.

The autumn gales had stripped the trees and hedgerows bare and the landscape now looked very wintry indeed, with temperatures plummeting as the air moved in from the north, bringing with it frost and 'snow on the hills', as the forecasters were so keen on saying.

Rats are well-armed creatures!

Winter

Gary had two useful terriers in Jock, the Middleton bred Lakeland, and Red, his rough haired fell bitch, which, though a good enough bitch at her work, was just a little too long in the back for me. A little bit of length in the back is desirable, though not too much, just as a short coupled terrier should not be too short in the back. Agility suffers with extremes and a well-balanced type is what is best suited to both work and the show ring. Some terriers are that long in the back, especially some so-called Jack Russells, that I am sure they can see their rear disappearing below ground as their front end emerges! Back problems can only result from such a build.

Gary and I were out on a rather cold winter day in search of foxes that were preying on the game birds belonging to a shoot syndicate and Crag marked the large earth as occupied. We had searched high and low and, as usual, hadn't found a fox until well into the day. We had a few more places to try and at last things were looking up. I fitted the locator collar and loosed my terrier, which sniffed at the hole and then disappeared below, after scratching away a little of the loose soil around the rather tight entrance. Gary stood back a little with Tiny, not exactly knowing where to put the lurcher, as there were several exits from where Reynard could bolt. It was some time before Crag finally found his quarry and now his eager baying could be heard as we waited in silence and keen expectation. Our fox was on the move and it erupted from one of the exits at a rapid rate. It ran across the pasture and headed for a small wood just ahead, but Tiny was loosed from the slip and was away, bounding across the field and gaining on his quarry all the time. Just before Reynard dropped into a ditch, which led to a brook bordering wood and pasture, Tiny struck and had his quarry, and there was no way he was going to let go now. The fox was a vixen of good size and in good condition and had no doubt fatted herself on the large pheasants to be found in this area. The keeper was very pleased indeed, not to mention the local farmers, and we went away from there having held onto our valuable permission for a good deal longer. There is nothing like good results for hanging onto permission. Though things didn't always go so smoothly.

I can remember an incident years ago when a fox took its chance and slipped away unseen. I was with Barry, a friend with whom I did plenty of digging throughout the 1980s and he was a veritable human JCB. Anyone would have been pleased to have had Barry on board when a fox was to ground and I have seen him create a cave in a hillside in the matter of a day, when helping to rescue a trapped terrier, shifting tons of rock, clay and boulder and opening up a massive hole right into the earth, and all without the aid of machinery, just using pick, spade and crowbar. Barry had Laddie, his rough haired Bedlington bred lurcher, with him that day, as well as Toby, a Nuttall type of Patterdale, and Suzie, his Jack Russell. And I had out Bess, my Greyhound, Merle, Rock and Pep. Pep and Suzie were hunting ahead of us as we traversed a narrow valley behind the huge swell of moorland and all of a sudden the pair disappeared into a drain which we were not previously aware of.

The pair spoke, telling us of occupation, but then fell silent as their quarry was on the move. I caught a glimpse of one of the terriers above and Merle and Bess were off, running up the hill and out onto the top pasture. Our fox had bolted almost immediately the terriers had disturbed it and it had chosen the top exit hole as its means of escape, which was out of our range of vision. The motley pack of dogs hit off the line and hunted it across the fields and out onto the moor, but Reynard was long gone and secured his brush for another day. This sort of thing has happened on quite a few occasions, for I enjoy having my terriers loose, in order for them to hunt and cast for scent. So sometimes they discover a freshly dug earth, or a drain I hadn't previously known about, and a fox usually gets away in such situations, when I and my bobbery pack are unprepared.

A similar thing happened when Gary and I were out at the Wilkinson farm, checking over a few earths to be found here. One of the best was a stone drain on top of a hill, which led along a large dry-stone wall, from a small duck pond in the middle of the hill pasture. This den is rarely dry, but there hadn't been much rainfall of late and the pond was far from overflowing, so no water had been running into it for the last few days at least. Rock was keen and I let her go, but kept Snatch on the couples. She had seen a few by this time and one of her best days was when she bolted three foxes from a dug-out rabbit warren alongside Ghyll, after they had got to ground together because I didn't know the earth was there. I was checking along a brook for rats, when they suddenly disappeared. I searched for them and found them baying in a three holed earth by the side of the stream. Three foxes then bolted, one after another, before the terriers emerged and went off

Rock & Bella marked keenly at a hole on the bank.

hunting them. She had joined in when flushing quite a number from covert throughout the autumn months and had made good progress. But this was a very long drain and I felt it best to enter a more experienced terrier.

Rock went like wildfire and she scrambled up the tunnel as keen as mustard. She began baying and Reynard shifted immediately, for Rock was no soft touch and could shift even reluctant foxes run in by lurchers, let alone one that was fresh and undisturbed. The old bitch began going wild with excitement at one spot and I wasn't sure whether or not our fox had decided to stand its ground and make a fight of it, so was distracted for a few seconds. In the meantime Reynard bolted at the exit and shot under a small gap in the huge wall cutting through the pasture, with Tiny left far in the rear, unable to carry on pursuit. Rock had kicked up a fuss because she couldn't get through a part collapse in the tunnel, which was much more easily negotiated by the slender fox, going crazy with frustration and anger.

We hadn't thought for one moment that our quarry would have got away in such a manner and by the time Tiny got over the high barrier, Reynard had sneaked away and secured escape. Rock continued to kick up a fuss and I couldn't get her to go back the way in which she had come, for she knew her quarry had gone through there and she was determined to do the same. And so what had looked like a simple operation now turned into a rescue and I returned to the farm for digging tackle. I cut a square of turf and dug down the couple of feet depth without too much trouble, opening up a hole by clearing soil away from where a stone slab had cracked and fallen into the tunnel, partially blocking it. Rock was a little large in the chest and she just couldn't follow her fox through. She scrambled out and was off, picking up the scent and going away on the line. Too much time had elapsed, however, and it wasn't long before she returned, rather disgruntled. Rock had been trapped to ground on several occasions and she was now towards the end of her career. True, she wasn't exactly trapped on this occasion, but I was certain she would have remained at that collapse and tried to get through until doomsday if I hadn't dug her out. I wrote a poem several years ago to commemorate one three day rescue involving this bitch and it goes as follows:

Reynard played happily on that early spring morn',
Not ever knowing danger since he had been born.
We sent Rock and Rusty to change things now,
To bay and to guide us, with shovels, that's how.
Baying and biting and dodging his teeth,

Telling where he lay in that tunnel underneath.
They stayed, they fought, they tackled him hard,
With terriers so furious, Reynard was on his guard.
With daylight fast fading, we were all worried sick,
But couldn't do much, with shovel, or with pick.
At first light next day, all the lads were there,
To get those dogs out of that dreaded, deep lair.
We dug, we sweat, we cursed and we swore,
And then Rock walked free, which we were grateful for.
But, with Rusty still jammed in that rock far below,
We carried on digging with a mighty heave-ho.
With this the third day that he was to ground,
We looked and we listened, but there was no sound.
So, with things looking bad, we thought our worst fear,
Then Rusty walked out, to a loud hail and a cheer.
With Rusty now at home, all safe and all sound,
We went and drank beer, till we too went to ground!

That had been one of the most difficult and taxing rescues I have ever taken part in and we tunnelled into that hillside for several feet, attempting to rescue the pair which were undoubtedly trapped due to fox carcasses blocking their exit. Rusty was a Buck/Breay bred terrier and no fox could live with him. Rock was young at the time, still learning her trade, but she worked superbly that day and a few bites showed she had joined in the action with great eagerness indeed.

Rock and Pep took part in the rescue of Crags, another Buck/Breay type of terrier descended from the Black Davy line. She had entered a rock earth and nothing had been heard for a long time. The owner asked a few lads to help out and, of course, we were happy to do so. I commemorated this rescue in verse too, but, unfortunately, it wasn't as successful as the rescue of Rock and Rusty. The poem reads as follows:

One early morn' in '85,
Charlie was on his rounds.
Little did he know, the terriers, they were there,
To bolt, or finish him, underground.
Reynard searched for a place to hide,
Deep down in the rocks, far below.
But Crags was there to seek him,
And seek him, she did so.

What happened then in that dreaded earth,
No one can really say.
But we dug, using pick, shovel and bar,
To shift that rock, soil and clay.
More earth dogs were entered, and tried,
Of the best and the very gamest kind.
Searching for Crags, through that deep, dreaded lair,
Herself and her quarry to find.
Rock and Pep went in, as well as Zak too,
To find that 'laal' bitch and to show her the way.
But still we don't know what happened,
From then, down to this very day.

Losing a terrier must be one of the most awful of things that can happen
to a terrierman. When one thinks of all the hours of toil that go into raising
a puppy; training and socialising it and finally starting it at its true vocation.
And then seeing it blossom into a good, if not great, worker. Then losing it
to ground and often not knowing what has happened to it, as in the case of
Crags, who was never seen again. It must be awful, to say the least. I am glad
to say that I have never lost a terrier to ground, though I have come close on
a few occasions, and they have been unpleasant enough.

One of the worst places where Rock was lost was in yet another rock earth
on the edge of an old quarry. Rock had been in for hours and I couldn't get
a mark on the locator. Many will not use a collar in rock and I must say I am
very hesitant myself, for there is always a slight risk of the collar catching as
a terrier pushes through tight spaces. It has been known for a terrier to hang
itself 'twixt two rocks in such situations, though that is a rare occurrence
indeed. Sometimes I have used a collar and at other times I think it best not
to do so, but this was not a rockpile, but a split in a crag and sound cannot be
so easily heard in this type of earth. Even deep terriers can usually be heard
in more hollow rockpiles, but this went right under the earth and I felt it best
to put on a collar.

I then put Bella in with the spare collar fitted, but felt rather dismayed
when the fifteen-foot mark disappeared within seconds. A collar was useless
in such a vast and deep place and so I put away the box and awaited the
return, hopefully, of both bitches. Bella wasn't long in returning, which told
me Rock blocked her way to the fox, but there was no sight, or sound, of her
mother and darkness fell soon after.

Tim and I returned with torches and continued to try to hear the bitch, calling for her to come out, but, without a mark, digging operations were pretty futile, though I doubt we would have got very far at this spot anyway, for it was pretty much undiggable.

It was a waiting game and, sure enough, Rock emerged two days later. She looked at me, just making sure I was still there, then turned around, intent on going back to her quarry which I was sure was on a ledge out of her reach, for she had no bites around her muzzle. I moved like lightning though and was too quick for her, diving to the ground and grabbing her back leg before she disappeared into the dark depths of the earth once more. She wasn't at all pleased, but I wasn't going to let her back in there and now keep terriers out of this huge place altogether, for when foxes can get out of reach in such circumstances they will never bolt, no matter how vociferous a terrier sent in to try. I thought she had got herself trapped, but obviously she was just staying with her quarry, attempting to get at it as it lay beyond her reach, taunting her, no doubt, and spitting defiance at the belligerent little earth dog. I have discovered one or two such earths during nearly thirty years of hunting the Pennine chain and foxes rarely, if ever, bolt from these strongholds. They know where they are safe and every pack of hounds will have its share of places that are best avoided. Some have been stopped by the terrierman, when possible, though many of these places are in rockpiles and stopping them is utterly impossible, for there are several entrances and exits.

Gary and I had been out all day and we had one last place to try. The large gorse coverts proved devoid of foxes, though on our last visit a large fox had been flushed from here by Ghyll and Tiny had coursed it across the rough scrub pasture. The tussocks of hardy hill grasses and dense patches of rushes, of course, Reynard used to the full in order to throw off his pursuer. Just as the lurcher was bearing down on it, the fox dipped under a wire fence and disappeared among the deep heather. We searched every earth within the vicinity, but found nothing.

It was that deep heather that we now tried and, sure enough, a fox was quickly afoot. Scent was everywhere and this led the pack of terriers on a merry dance, though Rock got away on the line and pushed her quarry out. A small, slender fox ran right passed me and then it headed downhill, with Rock close on its heels and baying for all she was worth. The rest of the dogs were round the other part of the heather and, by the time they responded, Rock had disappeared, with our quarry leaving little scent. We had enjoyed copious amounts of rain of late, which isn't unusual in this part of the world,

Rock, was trapped to ground several times.

We went and drank beer, till we too went to ground.

so scent wasn't lying too well on the sopping wet ground. The pack returned, but Rock didn't and a search was made. We eventually found her baying to ground in an old stone drain on the edge of a wood and I headed to the farm for digging tackle.

I returned with two spades and a pick and Gary and I were soon in action, cutting out quite a large square and digging down quite easily, which made a welcome change. Few digs are easy in this area and most are back-breaking. However, the soil broke up quite easily and we made good progress, breaking through some time later and accounting for our quarry – a small vixen in good condition, which had given a good account of itself. Rock had now worked well over two hundred foxes during her career, with numbers being nearer the three-hundred mark, if not over, but I could see she was struggling to cope with digs especially. And so, with a heavy heart, I resolved to retire her at the end of this season. Fox bites became more easily infected too, as well as taking longer to heal, so I thought it best to stop the earth work in particular. I could still use her on occasion for flushing foxes from covert, though I knew I had to be careful not to enter her at places where an earth may be found to be occupied.

Knowing exactly when to retire a working terrier is something I always find very difficult. Bites becoming infected more quickly and easily, despite your best efforts at keeping them clean, is one way to tell that a terrier is getting beyond its best. An older terrier may also be stiff for a day or two afterwards, especially after a long stint to ground, again taking longer to recover, with joints seizing up. A dose of cod liver oil everyday may do much to alleviate such problems, however, at least for another season or two.

An older terrier may get more than a little silly about rabbits. The professional terrierman will not usually work his terriers on rabbits, for they are exclusively used for foxes, but I have always used mine for rabbiting and can easily call them away from a burrow if I am after foxes. The hunt terrierman may find his older dogs showing interest in rabbits and even turning to them, instead of their more traditional quarry, when put to ground in order to bolt a fox.

This reminds me of an acquaintance of mine who travelled down to Cheshire and entered his ageing Jack Russell into a likely looking spot. This terrier was a superb fox dog and served with hunts during his career, but he later took more than a passing interest in rabbits. On this occasion his master dug several feet into the Cheshire earth and uncovered the terrier, which was baying at, and digging onto, rabbits. This sort of thing could easily happen to anyone who puts an old terrier to ground. In my case I find older dogs more difficult to call away from rabbit burrows and they will sometimes get in and bay as though they are on a fox, which can make things a little difficult. My old dog, Fell, is now in his ninth season (at the time of writing (winter '06)) and, though still more than capable of finding and finishing foxes, he has become a little bit silly about rabbits, being keener to dig on to them. This presents certain difficulties when working earths, but also when in covert, for he can get in a rabbit hole and then attempts to dig on, while baying.

On more than one occasion of late I have been forced to fight my way through covert in order to pull him out of a rabbit hole, reprimanding him whilst doing so, but realising it is a symptom of advancing years. I do not wish to give the wrong impression, he remains a superb fox dog, having recently killed two foxes to ground, during separate hunts, but I can see that retirement, at least from earth work, isn't far away. It is always saddening when such times come around, which they inevitably do, for one has been working alongside that particular earth dog for years, maybe for ten or eleven seasons, having come to rely on it greatly. Also, to leave a veteran at home when going off with the younger members of your team is heart rending and I hate to hear the barking, whining and howling that always occurs when an old dog has to be left behind. It is important to get the timing of retirement right, for one must not be left with inexperienced youngsters who need an older dog to show them the ropes. Wild animals learn from the example and experience of their parents and so do young terriers. If they do not have their parents to show them the way, then any older dog will do, provided, of course, that it is a good worker and is not quarrelsome.

I try not to put two terriers to ground at any one time, though sometimes this is unavoidable, maybe because they are working undergrowth and find a previously unknown earth, getting to ground together, or maybe because it is a large rock spot. Two bitches will normally work well together, but it is not advisable to put two dogs in the same earth at the same time. Much has been written about the early pedigree Lakeland terrier and about how quarrelsome they were, but that simply isn't an accurate reflection of the breed.

True, they did become much more quarrelsome in later decades, particularly when fewer and fewer were actually worked and boredom and frustration kicked in, but during the days when they were regularly worked throughout the Lake District, several could be run together at the same time. George Henry Long, as well as his father, Peter, used the pedigree breed in bobbery packs that contained all different kinds of dogs, including beagles and foxhounds, as well as other terriers. Fights were just as rare as they were with the old fell strains, simply because they were worked regularly and thus were content.

During the time that Willie Irving was Huntsman to the Melbreak Foxhounds (1926-1951) he used two types of terrier at fox. A strain of crossbreds which he created by putting his pedigree Lakeland terrier studs onto Border terrier bitches and producing a race of sensible fox bolting and badger digging types (all of Irving's terriers, his crossbreds and his pedigree Lakelands, were descended from his famous Turk, born in 1930 and one of the gamest terriers in the fells at that time), and his pedigree strain which were usually put in when Irving wanted a fox finished underground, either at lambing time, or when a fox was 'run in' late in the day.

All of these pedigree dogs were entered to fox, even after he left the Melbreak to help run the Hound Trailing Association (he retired from the hunt at the age of 53 because he felt hunting hounds on foot was a young man's job. He was struggling to keep with his hounds and felt it was the right time to leave). Irving used two dogs to ground at the same time on some occasions and his famous Turk was no battler, for young dogs were entered to quarry alongside this dog, who was death to any fox that didn't get out of his way rather swiftly.

Irving also entered his terriers early, at around nine months of age, as did G.H. Long and many of the early Lakeland Terrier Association breeders. Gary Middleton continues to breed a race of terrier that is descended from the early pedigree Lakeland and these too, like their ancestors, have a reputation for early entering (Middleton's strain is descended from the Egton Lakeland, Rock, as well as Irving's Turk, through Arthur Irving's Robin). Turk was only just over two and a half years of age when he died of poisoning after picking it up at a wood near Lorton, yet by then he had become one of the best workers in the fells and had produced many litters of puppies, so he must have been entered to fox quite early on. Those early breeders never bred from an unentered dog or bitch. Few working Lakelands of today do not have the blood of Irving's Turk in their bloodlines and even Frank Buck used such blood, for he bought pedigree Lakelands from Arthur Irving, Willie's brother, which were descended from Turk, in order to improve type in his race of mainly black terriers.

Winter brought with it harsher conditions and, for those who hunt with hounds, longer runs on some of the fittest foxes in their country. The terrierman is busy at this time of year, with earth-stopping in particular, when his terriers will bolt numerous foxes from their dens during the afternoon before the next day's hunting, but also throughout the hunting day itself. A fox may go into country beyond the 'stopped' area and get to ground, or it may get into a previously unknown lair. The terrierman will be called for and it isn't usually very long before he is on the spot, his game tykes by his side, in order to bolt the quarry. Many Huntsmen and Masters are not the most patient of folk, so the chap in charge of the earth dogs must learn to keep in touch with hounds and be on the spot quickly when his services are required. If the quarry will not shift, then, if asked to do so by the landowner, the fox will be dug and shot. If livestock has been suffering fox predation in and around the area though, then Reynard will undoubtedly be dug out and shot, but if not, he may well be left to run another day. However, if it has been observed that there is something not quite right with the beast and it seems sickly, then it will be accounted for. Hunting with hounds and terriers is about keeping the fox population in check and ridding the countryside of sickly specimens that may pass on disease to others, not to mention they may also kill farm livestock in order to survive, simply because they are too ill to catch wild prey. And so, if such beasts are left, then proper fox control is not being carried out and such a pack is of little use to anyone.

Our own little pack of terriers, accompanied by a lurcher, or a gun, at times, had flushed many foxes from covert during the autumn months and we had also accounted for a few that were found below ground. Now that winter had well and truly set in we were finding far fewer foxes above ground and, because their lairs above were being disturbed, they began using earths more frequently. We had quite a time of it at the end of December, bolting some from earths and digging one or two that wouldn't shift. Rock was used a little less now that she was toward the end of her working life, but at one time she was stamina personified. One Christmas, in '86 I think it was, she was used on every outing and did some superb work. I was in the building trade at the time and, thankfully, the whole site was given a full two weeks off over the Christmas period.

That last day on site was rather slow moving and we couldn't wait to finish. A few jobs needed completing before we went off site and these were done for about one o'clock. The gaffer then called it a day and we all headed off to the nearest Inn where sandwiches had been laid on for us. The Plain Tree Inn at Turn Village, Edenfield, was the venue for our celebrations and they were rather hectic, to say the least. I downed about eight pints, as well as a number of whisky chasers, during that long afternoon and we were joined by several local farmers who sneaked in through the back door long after 'last orders' had been called. How I got home I cannot quite remember, but I missed an evening out with my friends because I fell asleep when I got home and didn't get up again until the next morning. I wasn't too disappointed, however, for holidays meant time to be out with my terriers and Rock had by this time entered well to quarry. She had learned her trade alongside my Russell bitch, Pep, whom I suspected was one of the early Plummer terriers that Brian referred to as simply Jack Russells at the time, and had taken part in quite a few digs by now. And so she had blossomed into a good finder and one that worked much deeper than the Russell. Pep was very good if the earths weren't too deep and she would stay all day, and often did, until dug out. But it was Rock who was now being used to bolt foxes from the deeper places, such as rockpiles and old mineshafts, which I worked at the time, before I learned better.

During our first outing Rock found two foxes skulking in the old mineshafts above Rochdale and she quickly bolted one of them, though she eventually pinned down her second at a spot under our feet, which was quite deep. The first fox bolted round the hill and easily escaped the attentions of the lurchers and Greyhound and Gary and I could do little under the circumstances, so we just watched our fox casually scamper away up the valley.

These shafts are huge and exits are far and wide, so it is impossible to cover them all and catching foxes was nigh on impossible here, unless Reynard emerged at one of the holes that were covered. Gary had shot one fox here though, after waiting outside and being fortunate enough to have his quarry bolt at exactly the right spot. A dig was now on the cards as Rock worked her fox hard, but it wasn't easy going and, before we had chance to break through, Reynard managed to slip away and we watched helplessly as he too bolted and ran off down the valley unmolested. These old shafts contain large tunnels that make it impossible for a terrier to hold a fox until dug out, so there was little Rock could do to prevent her quarry from escaping the dig. Again, our fox bolted well away from our location and easily slipped away. I wasn't too disappointed, however, for my young bitch had worked wonderfully well and had found and shifted two foxes from one of the most difficult of places.

I haven't purposely worked any old mine in years, not since those early days of working fell terriers (I worked with Russells and an occasional Patterdale before this time), but Mist and Turk, two of my current terriers,

A champion terrier belonging to Roger Westmoreland.
Buck used Irving's strain of Lakeland to improve type in his terriers.

Pedigree Lakeland blood is present in most modern fell terriers and has improved type greatly.

Colin Armstrong's hard working strain are descended from pedigree Lakelands.

got into this same place by mistake only a couple of seasons ago. These two didn't even know the shafts are there, but they put a fox up among deep heather on the steep hillside and followed the scent right to the mines, creeping into the dark tunnels after their quarry. When they didn't return I quickly realised where they had gone and climbed up to the old shafts. After maybe forty minutes or so, two foxes bolted from a distant exit and I watched them casually wander off together across the hill, in the direction of a distant wood. Mist and Turk emerged soon after, from the same exit, and I was able to call them back. I do not like to have terriers in old mines these days, for I worry about them getting trapped, or hitting pockets of poisonous gasses, so I was more than relieved to see them emerge safely. If a terrier did run into trouble in such a place, then there is nothing one can do to assist it.

A friend of mine, John, once had a terrier in these mines and it turned its attention to a badger that must have wandered into the place that morning. He could hear his game little bitch, Rigg, a terrier bred down from the old Buck/Breay bloodlines, really at her quarry and he could tell by the noises coming from within that a 'Brock' was at home and he despaired, for he knew she had no reverse gears and there was nothing he could do to assist her, except wait for her to return. The badger eventually moved off, harassed, but certainly not harmed, by the angry terrier, and, thankfully, she emerged some time afterwards. He told me her chin looked like a piece of raw liver when she came out and it took her more than two weeks to recover from her injuries. At another spot, a rock earth on the Lancashire/North Yorkshire border close to Todside, he entered Rigg alongside a Russell bitch that was very experienced at fox, and, again, a badger was home. Rigg was just learning her trade at the time and she tackled her quarry head on, while the Russell stood back and bayed, and emerged some time later with three of her teeth gone and a good few bites around her bottom jaw. That was her first encounter with 'Brock' and so she proved to be unsuited to badger digging, which was legal until the early 70s.

Badgers are very tough opponents and terriers must box clever if they are to survive at this game for long. Although badger digging is now illegal in the British Isles, this activity continues in America and France in particular and a badger dog must be game, but have brains too. Terriers must stand back and bay at badgers if they are to survive for very long and Rigg was certainly not of this type.

After Rock had bolted those two foxes from the old mines, she emerged with just a few minor bites and was again in action a couple of days later,

Badgers are tough opponents!

when her and Pep found a fox skulking in an old tip we had visited in the hopes of finding a few rats. The two terriers shot into the heap of rubbish that included old prams, fridges, bicycles, car parts, tyres and goodness knows what else, squeezing their way through the tangle of rubbish in an attempt to reach their quarry. We then dug by hand, simply removing the obstacles, and finally accounted for a large dog fox that could have found itself a safer refuge. Again, Rock, not to mention Pep, had worked wonderfully well and that dig lasted for three and half-hours. We were all worn out, but were on the hill again a couple of days later.

This time Merle marked a stone drain at the foot of a hill, which was close to a wood full of brambles. I entered Pep first of all and her strong steady bay soon signalled a find. Merle and Bess were stationed a little way behind the exit and we awaited the presence of our quarry. But Reynard wasn't for shifting and some time later the little bitch was baying just as strongly and in exactly the same spot. We thought about digging, but the hard frost of late meant that the ground was very hard for at least the first few inches and so decided to see if putting Rock to ground could persuade the animal to bolt. Besides, we had already enjoyed two quite hard digs in the past few days and wished for a bit of an easier day today.

Rock had been keen to get throughout and she now shot into that earth and got stuck into her fox with gusto. If this had been a dug out rabbit hole with very little room to manoeuvre, then I would not have had two terriers in at the same time. Instead, I would have called Pep out (if possible), before entering the other bitch. As it was this drain has plenty of room inside for two and the pair now ganged up on the fox and shifted it at last. It came out of there like a bullet from a gun and headed for the wood. Bess was a greyhound and she quickly and easily pulled ahead of the slower, bulkier lurcher, bearing down on her fox at great speed. Foxes are never easy targets in such situations, however, and Reynard awaited his chance. Just as Bess was about to strike, the fox turned sharply and made up some ground, while Bess worked hard to get back into her stride. Again she came bearing down on her quarry, but he just made it into a dense bramble thickett and was gone, right up through the wood, using every bit of cover to throw off his tormentors. Merle made better progress through here, but still, he couldn't match his foe for agility through difficult obstacles and Reynard escaped. The two bitches were out soon after their fox and they hunted it up through the wood, out the other side and over the pastures now devoid of cattle, which were in their byres for the winter months. The pair didn't return, however,

Winter means longer runs for hounds. (Lunesdale F.H.)

... and harder work for the terrierman.
(Phil Brogden of the Lunesdale F.H.)

Rock, towards the end of her career.

so we headed off in search of them, for they must have followed their quarry to yet another earth.

Merle picked up a scent close to a narrow ravine that drained the waters from the pastures above, making them accessible to livestock. He hunted up the ravine and then marked an earth under a farm track. In fact, this was a small causeway across the ravine that linked the pastures and allowed the cattle to be moved around in order to prevent overgrazing. And, sure enough, the two terriers were baying like crazy, with Pep up to her fox and Rock stuck behind, rather frustrated by the whole business. Ever since she began working below, Rock has soon emerged in search of another way in if she couldn't quite get to her quarry and this always provided a chance to get a hold of her when another terrier was to ground. Sure enough, fifteen minutes later she was out, eagerly seeking another entrance, and I grabbed and shackled her. Pep was hard at her fox, baying steadily, and so I headed off to the farm for digging tackle.

We were rather limited in the amount of ground we could dig and I was happy, after quite some time, to break through quite close to Pep, being able to call her to me after more than a little 'persuasion', but getting to the fox was impossible. It was under the structure and we were forced to leave it for another day, as digging out the farm track would have been the quickest and surest way of losing our permission and of probably ending up in court for criminal damage. We back-filled the hole and left.

Our next outing saw us find a fox at yet another stone drain and this wouldn't bolt to the waiting running dogs, so, again, we had to trudge to a nearby farm for digging tackle and very soon afterwards we were cutting a square in the turf and beginning to dig down. Our fox stood its ground and Rock worked it really well. When we broke through, however, Reynard decided it was time to vacate the premises and made for the exit being guarded by Merle. A big dog fox was out of there before Merle realised it and it had gone a surprising distance before he began to gain on his quarry. The pasture proved good running ground for the lurcher, though, and he had it soon afterwards. I was on the spot shortly after he had caught his fox and I finished it as humanely and as quickly as possible, before allowing the terriers to have a taste of the carcass. And they partook most willingly, it has to be said.

The final venture of that holiday saw Rock discover a new earth at the foot of a steep hill, which led under quite a large boulder. She shot in and soon afterwards was drawing a dead fox out of there. She hadn't killed it.

My guess is, it had been shot and wounded and had later died in this earth. Its scent was still quite strong and to the terrier bitch it had been an easy, if puzzling, victory. I threw the carcass into what remained of a tangled mass of bracken and covered it over as best I could, before moving on.

As the terriers were drawing brambles above a small wood in a deep-cut valley, Rock shot to ground inside a dug out rabbit hole and began baying furiously. I managed to stop the others from getting in and, as I was attempting to shackle them and before we had got ourselves organised, out shot a large fox, a dog I would say, making off downhill, through the bushes and trees, and succeeding in throwing off its pursuers. I watched as it headed up the opposite hill and crept into the old mine workings. Rock, of course, wasn't far behind and there was nothing I could do to stop her getting in. Chris and I were soon on the spot and he put his dog, Zip, into the shafts in order to assist the bitch, for she wouldn't be capable of finishing such a large fox. Eight hours later, now dark and extremely cold and frosty, the two terriers emerged and Zip had undoubtedly finished his foe, for both terriers showed signs of having been hard at their quarry. We headed for home and got them fed, cleaned up and bedded down. It had been an incredibly busy fortnight for my fell bitch and she had worked wonderfully well. That was back in her younger days when she could cope with a heavy workload and it was sad to see that hunting forays were now really taking it out of her.

Barry was often my digging partner and one had to get out of his way rather swiftly, as he would bury anyone nearby in no time at all, he was that eager and that quick with a spade! My other digging partners included Chris, Gary, Carl and Roy. I hunted with a number of different folk over the years and have had some wonderful digs, as well as quite a few disasters. On more than one occasion I have dug down through soil and clay, only to come upon huge immovable boulders after maybe three or four hours of digging down several feet, with the terrier directly below and well out of reach. In such circumstances there has been nothing else for it, but to leave the quarry where it was, waiting for the dog to emerge when it was ready, which was usually many hours later. Crag was once to ground in such a place and he settled on his fox at almost fifteen feet in depth. We could hear nothing for most of the day, but had a clear mark on the locator. Gary and I dug for hours, until it was almost dark, when we eventually hit something solid with our spades. We dug around the obstacle for as far as possible and nothing but a mouse-sized hole appeared 'twixt the massive rocks. Crag, now easily heard hard at his fox, was only a few feet below these boulders, but it was no use

Barry would bury anyone in his way.

even contemplating carrying on. We were beaten and compelled to give our quarry best, once Crag had emerged, quite some time later on.

Bess also took part in some superb hunts that often lasted all day long. Also, I would often go out lamping after midnight and carry on until dawn, with the lurchers and greyhounds then taking part in coursing rabbits on the way home and adding one or two more to the tally. People often complain that greyhounds have no stamina, but Bess enjoyed many a gruelling day, or night, out hunting and I cannot recall her ever struggling to cope with the workload, not until she got older and had to be retired. She was quite intelligent too and worked out how to open the oven door in order to steal the chicken nestling inside – put there for our Sunday lunch (see *Rabbiting – With Ferret, Dog, Hawk and Gun*, published by Crowood Press, for the full story). Like Merle, she also sneaked upstairs on occasion and got up to mischief.

I had acquired a white dove from a friend who had tried out, rather successfully it has to be said, a bit of taxidermy. The bird needed the eyes putting in and the feathers cleaned up and replaced in their proper positions and I took pains over getting it into good condition, then proudly displayed it in my bedroom. I came home one day and walked into my room and the surroundings had taken on a surreal quality, for it looked as though snow had fallen heavily indoors! And then I realised that the white covering over almost the whole of my room was actually the proud feathers that had once been so beautifully presented on my white dove. Bess had got into my room and had completely wrecked the thing, plucking every feather from its rightful place and shaking them everywhere. As you can imagine, I wasn't amused in the slightest and the greyhound, whom I thought looked guilty, slinking around the place when I came home, got rather an ear bashing when I caught up with her!

Winter wore on at its usual slow pace and the frost, snow and sometimes-heavy rain meant that little cover was available for foxes which wished to shun the many earths of the hills and valleys. And so it wasn't too difficult finding foxes to ground, especially at those places that hadn't been disturbed too often. Crag went to ground in a dug out rabbit hole on a steep bank and began baying soon after. This would have been an ideal place for Snatch to have a go, but she had returned to her owner who had then sold her, which I wasn't too pleased about, for I had got the bitch going and she was now working fox keenly, both above and below ground. As it was, this was an ideal spot for Crag. He went in and bayed and stood back from his quarry, which meant that I was easily guided to the spot, without bothering to get a mark on the locator, for he was only about two-feet down at the most and was easily heard directly underneath.

He was a grand terrier to dig to and would stay all day until reached. But he wouldn't have too long to wait on this occasion, for I was down to him after taking out just a few spades of soil. He stood his ground and kept Reynard pinned down while I cleared enough room to work in and then a fully-grown, and rather large, dog fox was secured. He was in fine fettle and too good a specimen to kill, so I allowed him to run another day and gave Crag a good run as he chased his fox away. This was the time of year when foxes pair up and begin courting, so I felt it only right and proper that this fine dog fox should get a chance to propagate his line, for it is such animals that usually produce the best offspring. I know one must kill healthy specimens at times, especially when livestock is being preyed upon, but this fellow hadn't troubled anyone and I felt it unjust to have ended his life, so he ran for another day and no doubt went on to sire a fine litter that springtime.

The trees were now beginning to show fresh green buds and the green stalks of the daffodils were pushing their way through the earth and upwards towards the ever brightening sun, heralding the imminent arrival of spring as the year turned full circle once again. Lambing calls would begin in another month or so and soon after it would be time to hunt mink again. But for now we were still after foxes and one of the most memorable days towards the end of that winter was when Rock went to ground for the very last time.

She had enjoyed a wonderful working life and had proven a superb all-rounder, being adept at rabbiting, ratting and foxing. She also had an aversion to hedgehogs and, though I tried my hardest to stop her, it was a bad habit of which I was never able to break her. She would kill them by biting through the spines, the painful spikes driving her on to ever-greater effort. Fell terriers seem to have an inbred hatred of hedgehogs and this is no doubt because this animal was once on the bounty list of the Lake District and terriers were used to locate and probably kill them. This was because hedgehogs take the eggs of ground nesting birds and probably kill and eat young chicks too. Many predator species were on the bounty list in the fell country and the early fell packs hunted a wide variety of prey, claiming the bounty on those species that were found on the list.

I was hunting in the hills again and decided to try some dense gorse at a steep valley in the shadow of a huge moor. Foxes were hardly found above

Terriers are essential for working foxes from earths.

Gary Hayes chocolate dog, Sam,
works with the Eskdale & Ennerdale F.H.

A terrier used with the Lunesdale F.H.

Pep, Rock & Merle.

Bess.

ground now, though gorse seemed to be the exception. I hadn't been here for a while, so this covert may not have been disturbed for quite some time. In went Ghyll and Rock and soon after they were speaking, heralding that a fox was indeed skulking below the thorny branches. They chased it around for a while and then fell silent, so I skirted the gorse and listened intently for any sound, no matter how slight. I detected a faint muffled baying and knew then that they had followed their fox to ground. I managed to crawl under the dense growth and soon found the earth, which wasn't far from the edge of this covert, but digging was going to be difficult indeed. I could hear the terriers hard at their fox and it then decided to get out of there and bolted soon after, which I was rather glad about. Rock and Ghyll weren't far behind and off they went in pursuit, chasing their quarry out of covert and down the valley for quite some time and distance. When I finally caught up with them, I found that Rock had been quite badly bitten and so got her home and cleaned up as quickly as possible. That, I decided, was her last stint to ground and I promptly retired her that season. I was greatly saddened by this, but I did have other very good terriers to fall back on and Ghyll was shaping up to be something very special indeed. He was bred down from Breay's Bingo line, through the dogs of John Parks, and was living up to such breeding.

It had been a superb season and the bunch of earth dogs had put on a good show throughout, which rather pleased me. However, with spring just about arriving, it was time to hang up the boots and call it a day for another season.

Jim Dalton and Blencathra F.H. (1920s).

Jim Dalton, close to retirement.

Rock, retired after a hard day.

Joe Bowman's funeral. Fellback Huntsmen often claimed bounties on predators.

Rock hated hedgehogs.

Irving's famous Turk in 1931, with Cup won from a points system.

The Melbreak at Loweswater,
W. Irving, Huntsman, left, and Harry Hardasty, whipper-in, far right.
Note the leggy, typey pedigree Lakelands of the late 40s.

An early photo of Willie Irving exhibiting a typey pedigree Lakeland at Rydal Hound Show.

Joe Bowman with Ullswater hounds and a terrier displaying much Bedlington about it (foreground).

The Scottish breeds were once outstanding workers.

Cyril Breay with Rusty and Doreen Westmoreland on Leck fell.

Fell terriers serving with a fell pack, possibly Lunesdale or Ullswater. The Lakeland type on right is a type produced by Anthony Barker, while the one on the left is obviously from the Buck/Breay strain.

Tommy Dobson with 3 of his working fell terriers. Irving's strain, along with most others, had its roots in Dobson's terriers.

Spider being rescued in the Langdales in January 1934. Ran fox in at Cat Lugs, Langdales, on 30th January. 3 Terriers put in and rescued only 1, Spider, after 6 days. She was a Coniston hunt terrier walked by Mrs. Duder.

Cyril Breay (left) and Roger Westmoreland with Buck/Breay strain Lakelands.

Billy Irving with a group of his working pedigree Lakelands;
the Melbreak kennels are in the background.

Tom Meagean's 'Mockerkin' Lakelands. Alf Johnston was his kennelman during the 20s & 30s.
Note the good quality black & tans showing obvious Welsh ancestry. The 1st terrier in 2nd group
on right would easily pass for one of Gary Middleton's modern working Lakelands.

Anthony Chapman with possibly his best terrier, Crab, a near replica of the old type Welsh terrier.

Willie Porter with E&E hounds
and early Lakeland terriers at
the Angler's Inn, Ennerdale,
now under water after flooding
by the water authorities.
(ph. c.1900)